The Steadfast Stream

The Steadfast STREAM

An Introduction to Jewish Social Values

Arthur Lelyveld

The Pilgrim Press
Cleveland, Ohio

The Pilgrim Press, Cleveland, Ohio 44115
© 1995 by Arthur Lelyveld

Biblical quotations are from the *Tanakh: A New Translation of the Holy Scriptures According to the Traditional Hebrew Text* (Philadelphia: Jewish Publication Society, 1985). Variations from the JPS version are by the author.

All rights reserved. Published 1995

Printed in the United States of America on acid-free paper

00 99 98 97 96 95   5 4 3 2 1

Library of Congress Cataloging-in-Publication Data

Lelyveld, Arthur J., 1913–
   The steadfast stream : an introduction to Jewish social values / Arthur Lelyveld.
     p.   cm.
   Includes bibliographical references and index.
   ISBN 0-8298-1023-4
   1. Judaism and social problems.   2. Social values.   I. Title.
II. Title: Jewish social values.
HN40.J5L45   1995
296.3'87—dc20   94-39947
                                                                CIP

To Teela:

from the Hebrew Tehillah—:

a psalm, a song of praise,
a poetic expression of reverence,
a joyful lyric—
and Teela is all these,
blessed be the name

Let justice roll down like water

And righteousness like a steadfast stream

Amos 5:24

Contents

Acknowledgments   xi
Introduction   1
1. Values Are Not Vitamins   7
2. From Tabu to Divine Presence   19
3. Are All Created Equal?   33
4. Value Conflicts in Jewish Thought   43
5. From Rhetoric to Practice   63
6. A More Perfect World?   75
   Epilogue   89
   Notes   93
   Bibliography   115
   Index   121

Acknowledgments

I am indebted to many individuals and associations for their help in bringing this material to the point of publication. Much of the preparation and writing was done in the peaceful and scholarly ambience of the Oxford Centre for Post-Graduate Hebrew Studies in Oxford, England. The major impetus came from the Department of Religious Studies at John Carroll University, which elected me to the Walter and Mary Tuohy Chair for interreligious studies for 1989 and committed me to the lectures that form the basis for this study. To its chairman, Dr. Joseph Kelly, and to all my colleagues I tender this word of deep appreciation. I am grateful, too, to Marcia Rothschild and Betty Benjamin, who put the manuscript in its several drafts on the word processor, and to Ellen Leavitt, the librarian of the Arthur Lelyveld Center for Jewish Learning. My thanks, too, to Betty Bosnick and to Julie Moss, whose help in the final chores was most valuable. Above all, I am grateful to my beloved wife, Tcela, who has been a constant companion in these studies.

Introduction

Many elements of Jewish social concern are generally known among educated people. Jewish responsiveness to philanthropic causes is an uncontested fact, and the participation of Jews in movements of social betterment has won wide recognition. At the ballot box, the preponderance of Jewish votes has, according to numerous surveys, supported those candidates who give promise of being proponents of human rights and of a just society.[1]

It is surprising, then, that aside from a few selections of excerpts from classical sources, almost nothing on this subject has found its way into scholarly journals or published books. There has been no adequate effort, so far as we know, to analyze in depth the origins of this social concern and the nature of the motivations that have shaped it, preserved it, and transmitted it.[2]

Have Jews been nonviolent—seekers after conflict resolution rather than confrontation—through most of their history because they have been powerless? What of the acceptance of force brought about by the rebirth of the Jewish state? Have assimilation and acculturation brought a weakening of those characteristics that have contributed to the distinctive Jewish value stance?

These questions and others deserve fuller exploration. The effort presented here is based on the conviction that there is in the Jewish heritage that which can be seen as "normative." True, one must "turn it and turn it again for everything is in it,"[3] as the tradition itself tells us. For almost every value judgment we may cite, one can find antithetical statements expressed by individual sages. Indeed, the commitment to record minority opinions is in itself an illustration of the openness and receptiveness that are the hallmarks of the normative Jewish stance. "Both these [judgments] and these [opposing judgments] are the words of the living God," says the Talmud.[4]

When one encounters harsh outbursts in rabbinic literature, one is brought up short before the statement is interpreted or considered in context or recognized as the intemperate explosion of one irascible individual. Of course, anti-Jewish writers have seized upon such outbursts. For example: "The best of the Gentiles should be killed"[5] and "Converts are like a scab on the body of Israel."[6] These are disconcerting—until we read that one Abraham the Convert (*Ha-ger*) regarded the latter statement as complimentary rather than opprobrious, for it meant that converts are so dedicated and devoted that they make born Jews feel inferior and uncomfortable.

But recognition of the wide variety of aphorisms and opinions to be found in the vast body of Jewish thought that has come down to us should not obscure the central line of development and affirmation. This book will explore that normative content and trace its relevance to the Jewish concern for truth and equity, integrity and peace, compassion and the goal of a just society. These add up to a "value stance" that is founded in and motivated by religious conviction.[7]

This is the view of Leo Baeck, the Berlin rabbi and scholar who became the sage and saint of the Theresienstadt concentration camp. In his introduction to the third volume of *The Teachings of Judaism*, he writes:

> *The strength of its social thought as here set forth is that it is not only ethical, but that it is religious. The fellow-man, whether he lives near or far from me*

is my neighbor. God created him as He created me. He speaks to him and hears him as He speaks to me and hears me.[8]

This, to Baeck, is the foundation of Jewish social thinking: the mutual recognition by human beings of their common humanity. "Your brother shall live with you,"[9] Baeck quotes, and adds that in this context the word "brother" embraces all persons everywhere.[10]

This book, then, is an attempt to validate Baeck's conclusion and the ethico-religious obligations that flow from it, attempting to define "value," to describe the Jewish "value stance," and to see how it appears in its application to the community, to interpersonal relations, and to our world.

As I embark on this task, I should make clear my bias. I believe that normative Judaism lays particular emphasis on social righteousness as that which defines its cult and its culture, its ethic and its relationship to the Divine. The complex diversity of the tradition does not diminish the conviction that there is in Judaism a central core of motivation and goal as well as a description of the way to that goal.

Judaism embraces the whole of life—both direction and obligation. The *meaning* of life is a fit subject for thoughtful discussion; but such discussion allows room for a wide variety of opinions. The responsibilities that human beings must shoulder are clearly enunciated and allow little room for deviation—*Kiddush ha-ḥayyim*, the demand to invest everything with the presence of God—because they demand responses to the totality of that which exists, cancels out any distinctions between "religious" and secular, between sacred and profane. Everything the pious Jew does—from the moment of awakening, when the hands are dipped in water and God is given thanks for life, to the moment of retiring when the bedtime *Sh'ma*, the affirmation of God's unity, is recited—should be attended by consciousness of the divine presence and the will to enhance it.

"But wait!" says one who knows the tradition. In the *Havdalah* ceremony that marks the separating of Sabbath and weekday, "don't we describe God as *ha-mavdil beyn Kodesh l'chol*, the one who makes a distinction between holy and profane?" This, I would respond, is a liturgical conceit found not infrequently in the literature. In actual practice, the esteemed response is to "sanctify the everyday." There is nothing so profane that it will not yield to Jewish vigilance, sublimated by pious intent into the realm of the sacred. And we are talking about the ordinary, the real, encountered in life as it is lived and dedicated to the fulfillment of a dream of human welfare and social good.

In some religions there are tendencies to turn away from this world. We dwell, we are told, in mere "shadowlands," and there is another world, another life, more real and compelling, in which our frustrations will be resolved and our protesting questions will find answers. The deemphasis of the here and now, with its call to rely on a promised and better future, has sometimes been derided and sneered at as "pie in the sky when you die," but it is a sober response to the besetting theological problem of evil. A kind of "theodical calculus" solves the problem: the righteous suffer in this world, they say, only to be rewarded in the "next"; the wicked prosper here, but they will receive after death the punishment they deserve.

Some religious responses—especially in Eastern religion—entail an attitude that immerses itself in a group-generated and tradition-developed unchangeable real that is mythologically represented, with authority grounded in that mythology. The often-discerned corollary is that life does not present a challenge. Rather, this kind of response offers an instrument of escape from the pain and suffering of a sorrowful and predominantly evil life.

Yet another mood is that of those who bring to their basic attitudes a severe secular pragmatism in religious clothing. Put yourself in harmony with what you see as divine and you will achieve the fulfillment of all your desires here and now—in this life and in this world. This is what some popular television evangelists hold out to their viewers. They themselves become exemplars and role models, flaunting their luxuries, their motor cars, their jewels. This is instant salvation that you, too, can have in return for a small contribution.

The "TV preachers" are but an extreme example of one age-old aspect of religion. Religion has frequently been a gimmick, an instrument for self-gratification. This is what Martin Buber described as seeking to make an "It" of the Eternal Thou that can never become an "It." When the effort is made to harness the power of prayer for one's own ends—witness for example the pregame prayer sessions of some U.S. football teams—it is seeking to use God, making God an "It." This can be seen in the attempt to manipulate nature in prayers for rain, for abundant harvests, for success in this-worldly endeavors—an archaic as well as a contemporary aspect of religious practice.

Now, admittedly, each of these tendencies can be found somewhere in the rich and multiform diversity of Jewish thought. But when we stand back and consider the impact that Judaism has had on its adherents—both historically and at captured moments within its flow—we know that there is something at work that has centralizing and refining power, something to which we can attach the adjective "normative." It is something that cuts through the imaginative constructions of the *aggadah*—the speculative and value-seeking aspect of the rabbinic literature, portraying the "world to come" and the destiny of human beings after death—and inevitably returns to the acceptance of human responsibility in *this* world.

It is something that can be said, without oversimplification, to find its focus in the concept of *mitzvah*, in which God commands and God's creatures must respond in righteous action. It is a concept that is the major overriding and organizing metaphor in all the varieties of Jewish thought and in the obligations of the individual. It means the divine demand to "perfect the world," to struggle for the elimination of selfishness, greed, lack of concern for others, corruption, violence and war. It is, in other words, the leap from individual priority into a worldview that holds the vision of a redeemed society and commits us to enlist in the cause of bringing that society about.

1
Values Are Not Vitamins

The Talmud tells a story about a first-century pharisaic teacher who, despite a saintliness verging on heroism and an erudition demonstrated by the fact that the great Rabbi Akiba was one of his disciples, is accorded only a few references in rabbinic literature. His name was Nahum, and he probably came from the village of Gimzu, but because he was in the habit of accepting everything that was laid upon him with the reiterated response *Gam zu l'tovah*—"This too is for the best"—he was known as Nahum Ish Gam Zu. In his last years, like the biblical Job, he was in horrible agony: blind, quadriplegic, and stricken with boils. His disciples, seeking to bring him comfort and to remove him from his dilapidated surroundings, said to him, "Master, since we know you to be a *tsaddik gamur*, a wholly righteous person, why has all this happened to you?" He replied: "I brought in on myself. Once I was journeying on the road to the house of my father-in-law and I had with me three donkeys. One was loaded with food, one with drink and one with all kinds of dainties. A poor man stopped me on the road and said "Master, give me something to eat." My reply was, "Wait until I have unloaded something from the donkey." But while I busied myself with unloading, the poor man died. I then went and prostrated myself upon him and cried, "May my eyes which had no pity become blind, may my hands which failed to reach out to you be cut off, my legs which did not run to help you be amputated and may my whole body be covered with boils."[1]

A superstitious horror story? Its setting is surely alien to our contemporary views on reward and punishment. Its dominant value, however, is the same as that reflected in the gospel parable of the good Samaritan.[2] The ethic of Jesus and the ethic of the Pharisees, paradoxically despite the gospel fulminations against the latter, are one and the same, emerging as they did out of the same tradition. "Do not stand idly by the blood of thy neighbor," says the Torah. Concern for one's fellow human is among the highest values. "Love your neighbor as yourself" and "Love the stranger as yourself."[3]

Do we feel guilty when we avert our gaze from the homeless on our city streets or "pass by on the other side" when we are approached by panhandlers? How do those biblical and rabbinic values affect our responses to the problems of hunger, poverty, and homelessness in our own time and place?

Similarly, how do we deal with conflicting statements and antithetical value judgments? For example, we are told by an anonymous sage that if someone comes to kill you, kill him first (*Ba l'hargecha, hash-kem l'hargo*).[4] But the Talmud several times affirms the absolute sanctity of the life of a fellow human being. For example:

> One came before Raba [prestigious head of the academy in Babylon about the year 200] and said to him, "The Governor of my town has ordered me: 'Go and kill so-and-so. If not I will kill you.'" Raba answered him "Let him rather kill you than that you should commit murder. Who knows that your blood is redder than his?"[5]

Is this simply a distinction between self-defense and premeditated murder or an example of the rabbinic concern for the "pursued" rather than for the "pursuer"[6]—or is murder condemned under any circumstances? Because the answers involve value judgments, they are neither simple nor easy to determine. We ought therefore to spend some time in the effort to understand what we mean by "values" and, subsequently, "social values."

What Do We Mean by "Value"?

Overuse can kill a word. By depriving the word of precise content, overuse diminishes its ability to communicate meaning. "Value" is such a word. From its prosaic presence in bartering, buying, and selling to its position in the world of philosophy, where it has been said to be the focus of a "concentrated rescue operation," it has many different meanings.

In the media and on many lecture platforms, values have been seen as therapy for the ailments of society. We have been told that we live in a value-shunning era that knows the price of everything and the value of nothing. Therefore, we must "teach values" or "restore a sense of values" to our public policy makers. One would think that values are social vitamins and that properly administered they will counteract delinquency, the drug culture, prejudice, violence, and all the other assorted evils that plague us.

But values are not vitamins and they are not words. Even value terms that seek to describe moral ideals require analysis. "Justice" is not a value. Rather, our values determine what we mean when in a specific situation we say "justice." Our values are the factors that determine our choices. They are demonstrated, made evident, by what we do. Every individual, every group, is motivated by its values. Our society cannot be said to be "value shunning." Its defects are generated by its values, which may often be ego-oriented, hooked on self-satisfaction or self-aggrandizement, or tied to the acquisition of wealth or power.

The problem of defining "value" on the academic, philosophical level has been a baffling and frustrating challenge. John Dewey, whose clear preferences were for democracy, freedom, and benevolent interpersonal relationships, sought to found values on an empirical-naturalistic basis. His disciples have not yet been able to agree either on an adequate definition or on the theory of how values are generated. Dewey himself asked, quoting a colleague, "how [can we] guarantee that different writers on 'value' are discussing the same subject?"[7] It was Dewey's view that the first task of value philosophy is to determine the "field" in which "events having value qualifications are located."[8] In other words, and in a seeming truism, values have to do with human conduct.[9] What one does in one's present situation is what requires observation and analysis.

"The man who says he deeply or intensely values some 'end,'" Dewey writes, "and then shows himself indifferent to, neglectful of the things upon which the 'end' depends is either a liar intent upon deceiving others or is badly self-deceived." Separating ends from means, he adds, can lead either to empty and impotent "ultimacy"—"so ultimate as to be unattainable"—or to fanaticism and "all the evils that result from acceptance of the theory that the 'end justifies the means.'"[10]

Dewey asserted that values can be experienced as "feeling qualities" just as we experience color and taste: red or green, sweet or sour. "Empirically," he writes, "things are poignant, tragic, beautiful, humorous, comfortable, annoying, splendid, fearful."

A difficulty in this is that these adjectives have shifting meanings. Rather than being empirically grounded, they elicit different "feeling qualities" according to the background, temperament, or cultural orientation of the individual. I have sat in theaters and movie houses and heard others laugh uproariously at scenes that made me uncomfortable. The eclipse of the sun may create in me feelings of awe or reverence before the splendor of the corona, but to a headhunter in New Guinea or any member of a prescientific culture, it may be simply terrifying. This suggests that the qualities of which Dewey speaks are not inherent in things but are found in the response of the viewer. "Beauty is in the eye of the beholder," says the old adage, and experience validates this as true.

This is what A. Campbell Garnett perceives and develops in his critique of Dewey's instrumentalist point of view. For Garnett it is inadmissible to reject, as does Dewey, the proposition that there are values that are intrinsic to the object, the event, or the moment.[11] Of course, there are moments about which we are moved to say, as did Faust, "Erweile doch—du bist so schoen." ("Linger, stay—you are so lovely.")[12] But, as Goethe understood, these moments do not linger. The experience of them is idiosyncratic: they are subject to the evaluation of the individual experiencing them. Instrumentalism, Garnett holds in this context, stops short "just as it reaches the threshold of the crucial questions." These questions are those that deal with the nature of what is really good and "the reasons why we should be concerned with social good."

"Good," says Garnett, "means something more than 'good for.' If it is the last moment of a man's experiences (and thus has no consequences for him), it is better that it should be a moment of joy and content than one of pain and disappointment."[13]

The task of value theory is to find an adequate ground for distinction between values that may be specious and bad and the ethical decisions that will lead to "right" choices. Can a clash between two value systems be resolved on the level of whether "men can live and live well"? Garnett holds, "The trouble with this 'solution' of the problem is that it solves nothing when one of the two parties decides it can live better by living at the expense of the other." And he adds that history reveals too many examples of this power determination and that this "solution" is still being chosen in our world.

What, then, is the source of the "spiritual insights" (Garnett's phrase) that will help humanity find a true solution? Where is the grounding for the values we prefer? Let me offer a homely illustration of this dilemma. I have watched the actions of an ant struggling across the flagstones of a terrace as it pushed a burden three times its own size and weight toward the anthill that was its goal. This was the apogee of "communal service," the performance of an assigned task. But the ant's actions were a supreme expression of clumsiness and awkwardness. It fell two or three times for every time it succeeded in pushing its burden over an obstacle. And yet it persevered.

On another occasion, I brushed an ant off the page of the book I was reading and the poor ant had the misfortune to fall into a spider's web. I watched with fascination as the spider slid down the thread of its web, skillfully grasped the ant, rolled it into a ball, and extracted the ant's life juices. This was adaptation and efficiency at their fullest. For some axiologists, this is the major determinant of value.[14] In this instance, the witness was the evaluator. The values in this scene are intrinsic to the natural order. But the evaluator responds to the situation by distinguishing good from bad. My own value sympathies were with the ant—diligent, struggling against unequal odds, the underdog and, finally, the victim. But if the Nietzschean exaltation of strength and efficiency are at the top of one's scale of values, that person's admiration and support would go to the spider. Certainly this latter reaction would be found in the supporters of Nazi ideology.

The question rises again: Are there absolutes against which to evaluate and on which to ground values or on which to base "ethical decisions"? In the biblical phrase, how do we "distinguish between the pure and the impure"?[15]

The multiplicity of contentions regarding how values are generated testifies to the absence of certainty in this field of thought. From the axiologist who is convinced that a science of values is possible[16]—that it is possible to develop an "axiological ideology"—to one who describes value as the "combination of vectors in a 'zusammenhang,'" to another who holds that values arise quite simply out of interest or to satisfy wants or needs—there is a plethora of pronouncements that are not at all relevant to a search for moral direction. To say that values arise out of interest begs the question of whether the interest is worthy of satisfaction. Equally circular is the contention of Ralph Barton Perry that value exists in the state of "harmonious happiness" such as that which can be found among Quakers in the "sense of the meeting." This neglects the fact that among Quakers there is an antecedent disposition toward harmony—a preexisting commitment.[17]

Others have defined value in terms that reflect Jamesian pragmatism. A thing is good, says Robert Hartman, when it fulfills its concept: a good hammer, for example, is one that drives straight and true.[18] Is adaptation the source of value? Is coherence? Is efficiency? Is there superior value in the spider, or in the ant?

Value has been said to inhere in enlightenment, in intelligence. But saints are not always erudite, and the scientists at Auschwitz yesterday and the "scientific creationists" in the United States today had and have among them the holders of doctorates from distinguished academic institutions. "The wolf is not less intelligent than the sheep," says Perry, "and the Philistine is not less clear-headed than the poet or the mystic."[19]

These are but a sampling of the conjectures about value found in contemporary value philosophy. Paul Tillich, for one, had little patience for them or for the effort to create a science of values. He held that values have an ontological status.[20] They may not be empirically demonstrable, but they are rooted, he held, in the structure of being itself.

Tillich contends that one of the main weaknesses of value theory is its subjective and relative character.[21] In most versions of contemporary value philosophy there is no anchorage for values—they can be turned or overturned according to preference. "There is no way to distinguish valid values from mere valuations," he concludes, "other than to show the root of a value in the structure of being itself." Stopping short of what he elsewhere calls "the Ground of being," he holds that ethical values "are commands derived from the essential nature of man" in which the "ought-to-be" is rooted. The ontological foundation of values is this essential nature of man. This leads him into the unsatisfactory conclusion that there is no external criterion for the validity of norms. They can only be subjected to the continuous criticism of experience, "not only the individual experiences but the experiences of mankind as they are embodied in its ethical traditions."[22]

Unable to take the step from the too-tentative and inadequately defined "structure of being" to an ontology in "the Ground of being" providing absolutes as a foundation, Tillich is left with that subjective and relative character of values that he himself characterizes as a major weakness.

The Judaic point of view takes that final step. Its value stance is rooted in the conviction that there are absolutes, written, so to speak, into the constitution of the universe, and that they provide anchorage for values that secures them against relativism.[23] In this connection, a significant contribution is made by Henry Margenau when he distinguishes between factual and normative values. A normative value has the sense of antecedent command—it is not merely the satisfaction of a want. It has the propulsive power of an "ought."[24] This concept of antecedent command is central in Judaism. The formative idea of *mitzvah* as demand and response is the essential core of Jewish religion: "this *mitzvah* which I command thee this day is not too difficult for thee . . . it is in thy mouth and in thy mind that thou mayest do it."[25]

If, however, normative value having "suasive force and regulatory power" is based on antecedent command, who is the author of the command? If there are *mitzvot*, who is the *m'tsaveh*—the commander? Margenau grapples with this question and holds it to be crucially important because "for a functioning value theory, the commands must engage commitment."[26] Those theories that have been favored historically with the greatest success, Margenau avers, are those in which the "author" or "authorship" is clearly known or accepted. Among them are ethical systems stemming from divine revelations where God is the "author" and systems of legislation where a monarch or a lawmaking body provides the commands. But Margenau, too, stops short of a definitive answer. "Religion," he opines, "seems to be outmoded as a source of values," and both legislation and jurisprudence are limited as well as attended by uncertainties. His conclusion is that validation of values is in the survival of the group dedicated to them. Choosing as a mode the Ten Commandments (despite its "repulsive simplifying features [sic]"), he asks us to "suppose a society to be established in which the code [the Ten Commandments] has been tentatively adopted by all citizens and in which there is negligible interaction with other societies; we must observe that society for a sufficient time [centuries, he says] . . . and see whether it survives."[27] Margenau comes close to offering in this a summary description of the history of the people of Israel and its codes—codes that we shall define as social values.

Recognizing then, the difficulty that besets the effort to find a commonly accepted definition of "value" or to secure agreement on the source of values and the manner in which they are generated, we return to Dewey's classification of them as "behavioral." They are that complex of factors—genetic, environmental, and cultural, among others—that motivates specific forms of conduct, that determines choices as well as evaluation of the choices and the conduct of others.[28] To that complex in an individual or in a group, the term "value stance" may be applied. It can be seen as a constellation of inhibitions, enthusiasms, compulsions, and abhorrences with which that which is present is approached or received.[29]

Normative values are largely group-generated. They emerge out of the historic experience—aptly named "traditions"—of persisting communities that affirm, refine, and recurrently renew their commitments to a hierarchy of worths, an inherited set of evaluative responses. They come, through the process of transmission, to present the image of a kind of societal or communal superego.

The value stance of a group is shaped from an initial commitment evolving through its experience. Thus the value stance of the Scottish people involves a certain measure of parsimony, but this is not necessarily a pejorative term, as Occam's razor demonstrated—Scottish thrift is not merely a subject for witticisms. The Scottish stance contains characteristics that are recognizable: spare, devoid of frippery, displeasure in excess. It is not "stinginess." It is a distinctive cultural response—"stance" in this context seems to me to be a well-chosen term. Related to the Italian *stanza*, it means a stopping place, a station, or a position. In the terminology of sport, it is the way golfers place their feet and position their body. The golfer's stance will in large measure determine the direction the ball will take: hook, slice, or down the middle.

This may be more than an analogy. Some older studies, which have since been confirmed, suggested that a "motor attitude akin to posture" *precedes* the feeling or complex of feelings that then conditions subsequent actions. "First we tense our muscles and assume an aggressive or defensive stance," wrote Nina Bull many years ago, "and then we feel 'anger' or 'fear.'"[30] It does not seem farfetched, then, to say that emotive or valuational responses are the products of a "posture" that has been conditioned by experience, environmental influences, or cultural background. We speak of a "disposition"—as when we say "He has a disposition to receive everyone cheerfully." Or we speak of people who are "open" in contrast to those who are "closed off," locked up in themselves and unresponsive—an adjectival usage that reflects the imagery of physical position—or, in another word, "stance."

The four-thousand-year span of Jewish history has formed a Jewish value stance that in its total *gestalt* exhibits a definable uniqueness. The task of describing that stance is attended by difficulties, not least of which is the tendency to select only its best aspects and develop a panegyric. But if values are the factors that influence decision making and are evidenced in the actions of the individual or the group, they are not a warrant for praise or blame of those who possess them. They hang on the luck of the draw.

There are normative Jewish values that constitute a distinctive Jewish value stance discernible in the group. But this group, like all others, has produced its fair share of scoundrels—deceptive or untruthful, violent or self-serving.

The consciousness of this all-too-human departure from the behavior enjoined by the nation's value obligations was present in the prophetic tradition. From Amos to Third Isaiah, the prophets of Israel excoriated their fellow Israelites who in self-centered indulgence placed burdens on the backs of the poor and the dispossessed. They did so in the name of God, whom they saw as the ultimate value commander. It should not be surprising that even today there is this kind of imperfection. It can be seen in a modern Israel basically split down the middle between those who proclaim "Peace Now" and those who would refuse to trade territory for peace, but also encompassing all of the possible positions between these two sets of convictions. Paradoxically, those who support the idea of Greater Israel do so on the basis of alleged biblical warrant and identify themselves as "religious" in the belief that they are carrying out the divine demand.

Nietzsche saw clearly the distinctive value stance I have posited only to denounce it as a "slave morality." His effort to subvert or "transvalue" the values expressed in the Judeo-Christian heritage, and often cynically or hypocritically deformed, can be judged by the fragmentation and misery it brought in its train and, by reverse twist, can be seen to validate what he sought to destroy. Value stance that eschews confrontation and violence has yet to find its validation in the way it affects interpersonal and intergroup relationships.

Additional testimony to distinctiveness can be found in the fact that value terms are untranslatable and that value concepts are indeterminate, or "multisignitive."[31] They are what Suzanne Langer called "charged symbols" —filled by the dynamic history of usage with layer upon layer of association.[32] Thus the value tone of the word "love" is not the same as that of the word *amour*. So, too, with the Hebrew word *Kadosh*, which usually is translated "holy" but possesses a linguistic distinctiveness that makes that rendering totally inadequate. The interrelationship between language and stance as it is seen in Hebrew value terms and expressed in their development will now be explored.

2

From Tabu to Divine Presence

In the preceding chapter, we maintained that values are not words. They are the complex of factors that determines our choices and forms part of a total value stance—a posture or a disposition from which we confront that which is over against us and to which we must respond. This having been said, we must admit that there is an inescapable connection between values and language. Every language has its own colors and nuances and expresses the value stance of the culture that produced it, and in turn the culture's values are shaped, transmitted, and preserved by value terms—that is, by language. This is what makes translation difficult and in some cases impossible.

A prime and instructive support for this assertion is the Yiddish language. Yiddish, which is basically the middle-high German that Jews took with them into Eastern Europe, preserves the Hebrew value terms and expressions of relationship in unique combinations. Professor Gershon Winer, chair of the Yiddish program at Bar Ilan University in Israel, has written that "Yiddish is so saturated with Jewishness that even secular Yiddish becomes a vehicle for Jewish religious values and for Jewish ideas."[1] Yiddish, interestingly, is remarkably free of curses and obscenities ("swear words"). Instead of cursing, speakers of Yiddish take refuge in tongue-in-cheek asseverations, such as "You should shine like a chandelier: hanging and burning." And "You should flourish like an onion: head in the ground."[2] It should be noted that this relative freedom from obscenity and blasphemy is also true of Hebrew: the early pioneer settlers had to borrow Arabic expletives from their neighbors before they developed their own. This can undoubtedly be ascribed to that respect for the power of the word that is initially manifest in the third commandment in the Decalogue and in the talmudic injunction[3]: *Ḥachamim hizaharu b'dvrei-chem* ("Sages, be careful with your words").

The preponderance of the Hebrew words retained in Yiddish are cultic or literary terms, the latter of which are primarily religious. They include value terms and terms of relationship. For example: the most frequently used Yiddish word for a good person is the Hebrew word *tsaddik*, and an evil man is a *rasha*. Slander is *lashon ha-ra*; wedding is *chasinah (chatuna)*, funeral is *levayeh*, circumcision is *bris*. All of these classical Hebrew words are examples of the persistence of Hebrew in Yiddish. Each of these terms, and others that will follow, is a "cluster word" that, as we shall see, requires interpretation.

The same phenomenon is found in Judeo-Spanish (Ladino) and, according to some observers, is rapidly developing in the English spoken among practicing community-oriented Jews in the United States.[4]

This preservation of Hebrew value terms is by no means a unique phenomenon. Arabic religious, literary, and cultic terms are preserved in Urdu and in Persian, and scholars of language could surely produce other examples. The significance of this lies in the fact that the terms retained are in reality untranslatable and are the shaping vocables to which we have already referred. This was the burden of a seminal paragraph in an address by Ḥayyim Greenberg to a World Zionist Congress when he said, in reference to the revival of the Hebrew language in the reborn state of Israel:

> *A Jew who can name all the plants in Israel in Hebrew or call all the parts of a tractor or some other complicated machine by their correct designations (in new Hebrew coinage) possesses one qualification for useful service in the State of Israel . . . But if he does not know to their deepest soundings and in their context of spiritual tensions such Hebrew expressions as* mitzvah, averah, ge'ulah, tikkun, tum'ah, tahara, yirah, ahavah, tzedaka, ḥesed, mesirut nefesh, kiddush ha'shem, devekut, teshuvah, *he cannot carry a part in that choir that gives voice, consciously or not, to . . . 'the Jewish melody.'*[5]

We shall have more to say about why none of these terms can be rendered by a single English vocable.

The key words in Greenberg's penetrative statement are "to their deepest soundings and in their context of spiritual tensions." Each term, in its etymology and in its usage, has a history that fills it with meanings.

Let me illustrate this contention by examining the word *mitzvah*.[6] *Mitzvah* is a noun whose root *tsevah* means, in its intensive form, "to direct" or "to command." In its simple form, it may have meant something like "to join together."[7] Indeed, it often has that meaning in rabbinic literature, where *mitzvah* is seen as the bond between God and Israel. In its biblical development, the term takes on a two-sided meaning. It is both God's command and the affirmative response to that command by human beings— the deed that carries out that command. "For this *mitzvah* which I command you this day is not too difficult for you," we read in Deuteronomy (30:14), "it is in your mouth and your mind that you may do it." The divine demand is the obverse of the coin, and the human action in response is its reverse. Using the word from its human perspective, the Talmud tells us, in a popular aphorism, "A *mitzvah* [the action] brings another *mitzvah* [action] in its train."[8]

According to tradition, the *Torah*—literally, "teaching" or "doctrine," not "law" (in this context the first five books of the Hebrew Scriptures or Old Testament)—contains 613 *mitzvot* that Jews are bound to perform to the extent that they can be performed (non-Jews have only seven).[9] Other actions that are not specified in the Torah, such as the kindling of lights on the eve of the Sabbath and similar ritual or cultic deeds, are regarded by the tradition as *mitzvot*. And a later authority, founding himself on early rabbinic interpretations, declares that "any act performed in accordance with the will of God is *mitzvah*."[10]

When in contemporary Jewish usage someone is enjoined to "do a *mitzvah*" (e.g., "It would be a *mitzvah* to go visit your grandmother"), it may mean a simple good deed, like a Boy Scout's daily good turn—but it achieves its full meaning when it is a response to ultimate demand, for it is that connection to an antecedent normative value that renders it "good."

This kind of development—the "charged symbol" aspect of value terms—can be seen clearly in the evolution of the term *kadosh* (usually rendered by the word "holy"), which carries us the full distance from *tabu* to the sense of presence that characterizes the response known as "religious" in all cultures and in many languages. Moreover, in a direct way that will become evident in what follows, the term *kadosh* is connected to and provides the motivation for ethical conduct.[11]

But whether the word is *tabu* or the *mana* of the South Pacific or the *orenda* of the American Indian, it testifies to an experience that is essentially ineffable. Rudolf Otto applied to it the word "numinous." The word *kadosh* also has the character of Otto's *mysterium tremendum*.[12]

In early biblical and Semitic pagan usage, the *kadosh* was an unseen power ascribed to natural objects such as sacred trees and pillars. That power was seen as dangerous—and frequently lethal: "Do not touch it, lest you die."[13] Only those who were properly prepared or authorized to do so could approach the cult object. When Aaron's sons, Nadab and Abihu, rashly drew near to the altar in the wilderness sanctuary without having been designated to do so, they died in the fire that they had erroneously brought. The *kadosh,* Moses then says, is to be dealt with only by those *(k'rovim)* who are appointed to that responsibility.[14]

The memory of that lethal power is expressed in the disturbing tale of an incident that occurred when David, having recaptured the ark of the covenant from the Philistines, was bringing it back to Jerusalem, twenty years after its mere presence had brought disaster on the people of *Beth Shemesh.*[15]

In that story, the ark had been placed on an ox-cart with the sons of Abinadab, Uzzah and Achio, as its drivers, and David, followed by a great entourage, accompanied it in a joyful procession with song and instrumental music. But this revelry was to be a setting for a tragedy. When they came to the threshing floor of a certain Nachon, the oxen stumbled and it appeared that the ark was about to fall from the cart. Uzzah, seeing what was happening, quite naturally put out his hand to steady the ark and immediately on touching it was struck dead.

This is a story that violates all our preconceptions about God. Gilbert Murray finds it particularly distasteful. Calling it "the deliberate act of an anthropomorphic God striking a well-intentioned man dead in explosive rage for a very pardonable mistake," he suggests that "a dangerous element has been introduced into the ethics of that religion." He concludes that "a being who is the moral equal of man must not behave like a charge of dynamite."[16]

However, the element of irresponsible divine anger that both Murray and we find unacceptable was not being "introduced" in the story of Uzzah. Rather, it was an element in a much older tale. Stories that preserve unsupportable ideas are found in all cultures. Medieval tales that can find no approval in "higher" or more sophisticated religious thought abound—such as, for example, the legend of Dr. Faustus, who, having sold his soul to Lucifer, is condemned by an unforgiving God to eternal damnation.

The ethical content of the *kadosh* was yet to be developed. How it grew out of the sheath of *tabu* can be regarded as one of the mysteries that abound in the realm of human progress, but it may not be too far afield to ascribe a crucial change to the genius of one man, Isaiah of Jerusalem, the eighth-century prophet whose revolutionary insight is expressed in the book that bears his name. A city man and member of a class that had access to the Temple and to the king, he experienced a vision out of which the single greatest motivating force of Jewish values was to emerge.[17]

Isaiah's concept, born in a vision attended, as he tells it, by the celestial hosts, was that the *kadosh*—the invisible and ineffable but powerful presence—was not to be found in cult objects or even in heavenly beings.[18] It was the Lord of Hosts whose glory or whose Presence (*Kavod*) fills the universe. This is what is ascribed to the *seraphim* in the vision as they call to one another: *Kadosh, Kadosh, Kadosh Adonay Ts'vaot, m'lo kol ha-aretz k'vodo*—"The Kadosh is the Lord of Hosts whose presence fills the world." Isaiah initiates the use of the phrase *"K'dosh Yisrael"* as an appellation for the Divine—the *Kadosh* of Israel—as distinguished from the *kadosh* of the nations round about.

That presence—the noun is *k'dushah*—must be invoked and established by the actions of human beings. This, too, was boldly proclaimed by Isaiah: *Ha-el Ha-kadosh nikdash bits'daka* ("God who is the *Kadosh* is made *kadosh* by righteous action").[19]

This is the kernel of the idea that was to grow and to blossom as it was transmitted to Isaiah's disciples and into the evolving value tradition. It finds a new focus in chapter 19 of Leviticus, in which the idea that human beings can participate in God's *kedushah* is projected. The declaration with which the chapter begins proclaims it: "You are *k'doshim* as I the Lord am *Kadosh*."[20] This becomes the topical sentence for a series of injunctions that, recognizing the divine presence in others, obliges us to respond to them with a proper respect for the presence, actual or potential. Rabbi Levi ben Yosef, a sage of the fourth century, states clearly what is implied by this belief: "Do not say, since I have been despised, I may despise my fellow-man—if you do this consider Who it is that you are despising—your Father in heaven," and he cites as scriptural warrant Genesis 5:1, which an earlier sage, Ben Azzai, had selected as the all-inclusive verse of the Pentateuch: "In the day that God created man, in the likeness of God, He created him."[21]

Experience tells us that this is a counsel of perfection. If God's presence is to be found in other human beings, it is sometimes deeply buried under layers of prejudice and hatred, erupting in brutality and scorn for the value of life. If the ideal toward which our normative values are to propel us is ever to be achieved, we must find our way to that hidden core of presence. In more prosaic terms, the task of behavioral scientists is to find the way to affect interpersonal relations by reducing self-interest and contempt and encouraging socially affirmative responses to flourish.

The value commands in Leviticus 19 are counsels of perfection, but they have provided a goal for human relations toward which to strive and to which so many have been committed through the centuries. What is remarkable is the fact that, counsels of perfection or not, they have received from Jews an incomparable degree of faithfulness through more than three millennia. The sages even boasted, attributing their words to King David, that the people of Israel were characterized by three traits: compassion, modesty, and deeds of loving kindness.[22] And *mirabile dictu*, it was a boast that was to conform largely to reality. This was a response to what was seen as the divine demand.

The commands in Leviticus 19 are punctuated in a kind of litany with the reiterated declaration "I am the Lord." This serves as a repeated reminder and suggests that the writer or writers of what has been called "The Holiness Code" was expressing a connection between God's *kedusha* and that which, inhering in human beings, demands their concern for the deprived. "Leave the corners of your fields and the gleanings of your vineyard for the poor and the stranger: I am the Lord your God." "Do not steal or lie or deal falsely: I am the Lord." "Pay your hired employees promptly, before nightfall." "Do not curse the deaf or put stumbling blocks before the blind: I am the Lord."

This latter injunction makes clear that the wrongdoing is disrespect for one's fellow. It is not only a concern for persons with disabilities that should motivate you to refrain from "cursing the deaf," because they cannot hear your cursing. Cursing them connotes a lack of compassion but also a lack of reverence for the image of God in the individual with a disability. Later we shall see how the command to refrain from putting stumbling blocks before blind persons is interpreted and expanded in the rabbinic tradition.[23]

The climax of this series is, of course, the great commandment: "You shall not take vengeance nor bear a grudge but you shall love your neighbor as yourself," which is further explicated before the end of the chapter with the words "the stranger that dwells with you shall be to you as the homeborn and you shall love him as yourself for you were strangers in the land of Egypt: I am the Lord your God."

For Rabbi Akiba, the command "Love your neighbor as yourself" was the *k'lal gadol*, the great inclusive principle of the Torah, although, as we saw above, Ben Azzai found an even more inclusive command in a verse that finds the divine presence in human beings (Gen. 5:2) "in the image of God created he [them]."

Other sages found other candidates for recognition as the *k'lal gadol*. Rabbi Nahman ben Isaac, for example, cited Habakkuk (2:4): "The righteous shall live by reason of his faithfulness."

This search for a *k'lal gadol* was evidently a favorite pursuit of the sages.[24] It is paralleled in the New Testament by Jesus' response to the challenge that he name the "great commandment"—the *k'lal gadol* that includes all the others. His response is: "You shall love the Lord your God with all your heart, with all your soul, and with all your might . . . and another like unto it: you shall love your neighbor as yourself."[25]

Hillel, an older contemporary of Jesus, head of the academy, a Pharisee and regarded as "the gentle sage," is the central figure in a similar story. A heathen had gone to his colleague, Shammai, with whom Hillel was "paired" in leadership. With supreme *chutzpah*, the heathen demanded to be converted and taught the whole of the Torah while he stood on one foot. Shammai, who was engaged in some construction project, drove him away with the builder's cubit that was in his hand. The heathen then went to Hillel and made exactly the same request. Instead of rejecting him, Hillel answered with the patience for which he was renowned: "What is hateful to you, do not do to your fellow human being. This is the whole Torah. The rest is commentary. Go study!"[26]

Hillel, it is clear, did *not* think you could sum up all the values and commands of the Torah in one verse or one aphorism. Every value command demands interpretation and requires understanding of the complexity of decision making. Even the great "Love your neighbor as yourself" has been the subject of multiple interpretations: indeed, a body of literature exists on that single *mitzvah*. A favorite example is the interpretation that says *V'ahavta l're'echa . . . Kamocha*—"Love your neighbor . . . he is just like you!" As in every value concept represented by cluster-words, the command to love involves a plethora of ideas that gives shape to the central concept.

This can be seen in the development of the two most propulsive ideas in Jewish ethics, both derived from the concept of *k'dusha*. One is called *kiddush ha-shem* (making God's presence felt), and the other is *kiddush ha-ḥayyim* (filling all of life with that presence).[27]

Kiddush ha-shem means the kind of human conduct

that defends, so to speak, the reputation of God. Each of us is, if it can be said without flippancy, potentially God's public relations person. The opposite of an act of *kiddush ha-shem* is *Hillul ha-shem*, which means injuring or demeaning God's reputation through unethical or immoral behavior. The supreme act of *kiddush ha-shem* is martyrdom.[28] An anecdote related in the Talmud illustrates the idea that *kiddush ha-shem* is an act that enhances the divine reputation. It is told of Shim'on ben Shetach, a sage who lived in the first century B.C.E. and was a leading Pharisee.[29] His disciples purchased a donkey from an Arab as Shim'on's agents. When they brought him the donkey and were grooming it, they found a precious stone in the donkey's ear. Overjoyed, they brought Shim'on the jewel and argued that under civil law it was rightfully his. "You bought a donkey, not a jewel," was Shim'on's response, and he told them, "within the line of the law," "Go and return it to the seller."[30] They did so, and when the Arab received it, he cried out, "Blessed be the God of Shim'on ben Shetach!"

The second and, you might say, twin concept is *kiddush ha-hayyim*. More than anything else and contrary to the popular idea of what is "holy," *kiddush ha-hayyim* takes *k'dusha* outside the cultic or "religious" setting and seeks to apply it to the whole of life—to mundane everyday activities. Consciousness of the divine presence should have a direct effect on conduct. Here we deal with a conviction that was first voiced by the prophets of Israel. Ritual without appropriate action is empty and inutile. The cry of the first Isaiah was "I cannot abide iniquity along with the solemn assembly . . . seek justice, relieve the oppressed," and the poetic reiteration of it by a later prophet of Isaiah's "school" was "Is not this the fast that I have chosen . . . to deal your bread to the hungry, when you see the naked that you cover him, and bring the poor into your house?"[31]

Paradoxically, despite the condemnation of ritual unattended by righteous action, it must be affirmed that ritual is a major instrument for the transmission of values from generation to generation. The freeing of the Israelites from

Egyptian slavery provides a motif that is voiced again and again in the liturgy of the synagogue and the home. The very first word of the Decalogue (Exod. 20; Deut. 5) announces the divine intervention in what has been celebrated through the centuries as the first historically recorded blow against tyranny. Again and again, the words "for you were strangers in the land of Egypt" provide a refrain and a reminder: "The stranger you shall not oppress, for you know the very being *(nefesh)* of the stranger, since you were strangers in the land of Egypt" (Exod. 23:9).

The reminder appears again in the Sabbath command in its second version—in the book of Deuteronomy.[32] It is repeated by practicing Jews every Sabbath eve and every festival eve when in the *kiddush* they raise the wine cup to invoke the divine presence and announce that the ceremony is in "remembrance of the exodus from Egypt." After every meal, in prayers of thanksgiving for the sustenance they have received from God "who sustains the entire world in His goodness" and provides that sustenance "to all created beings whom He has created," Jews make mention of redemption from Egyptian slavery.[33]

The dramatization of this idea in the Passover meal called the *seder* has undoubtedly been the most powerful instrument for the transmission of this memory. The telling of the story (in Hebrew: *haggadah*) is directed primarily to the children ("And you shall tell your child in that day . . ."). The youngest one present asks the questions that are to elicit the narration, and everyone present is required to identify with the Egyptian experience: "to look upon himself as if he himself had gone forth out of Egypt."[34]

"Dramatization" is the correct term, because the story has frequently been acted out for the delight and edification of the little ones. We are told that North African Jews would take staffs in hand and gird themselves for the epochal journey.[35]

The *seder* (the word means "order" and refers to the order of the ritual) actually begins with a universalistic proclamation that expresses its intent. The leader holds up a plate on which the major Passover symbols have been arranged—the roasted shank bone, the egg, the spring greens, the bitter herb—and proclaims:

> *This is the bread of affliction which our ancestors ate in the land of Egypt. Let all who are hungry come and eat; let all who are in need come and celebrate the Passover with us. This year there is slavery, next year [may there be] freedom. This year here, next year [may it be] in the land of Israel.*[36]

The central universal goal of Judaism and the matrix of all its social values is imbedded in the prayer that closes every communal worship service (daily, Sabbath, and Festival), known familiarly as *aleinu* ("it is our obligation"), calling upon us *L'takayn olam b'malchut shaddai*—"to repair or improve the world into the kingship of the Almighty." True worship of the one God, this prayer implies, will mean the ending of evil in all its forms.[37]

Ritual, then, is a constant reminder and support for major social values and a guarantor of their transmission—even to the point of emphasizing conduct contrary to the usual forms of human behavior. The "slaves in Egypt" motif illustrates this, because it does no less than turn the common human mechanism of projection on its head. "Projection" is the usual way in which we endure hurts or blot out the effects of humiliation. "Pass it on" is the injunction for this kind of behavior. Joe has had a bad day at the office—the boss has chewed him out—and so he comes home and speaks harshly to his wife, Sarah. She has had a bad day at work too, so she in turn snaps at their child and the child goes out and kicks the cat. First-year college students going through hazing can't wait to become sophomores so that they can mistreat the newcomers. These examples may be too pat, but I warrant they are recognizable. Jewish tradition commands the very opposite response. Because it has happened to you, you must see to it that it will not happen to others. "You shall not oppress a stranger for you know the very being of the stranger, you yourselves having been strangers in the land of Egypt."[38]

Command, application, and group survival—these are the factors that for Tillich constitute the major elements in the process of validation of values. And these elements, found in the ways in which Jews committed to the normative values of their tradition seek to act, condition the way in which those Jews approached their everyday contacts and everyday responsibilities.

With the yardstick of *kiddush ha-shem* (positive) and *hillul ha-shem* (negative), Jews have been able to achieve a consensus of measurement by which they may declare some actions to be "un-Jewish." Miserliness and greed are "un-Jewish." Delighting in violence is "un-Jewish": witness the rejection of such so-called sports as cock fighting, bear baiting, bullfighting, and hunting. By reason of their antecedent commands, Jews may not hunt either for "pleasure" or for food, the latter restriction deriving from the prohibition against eating any meat except that of humanely slaughtered and ritually clean animals.

Saul Bellow, in his novel *Herzog,* finds it almost inconceivable that a Jew should even possess a gun. "Violence was for the goy!" Herzog affirms. The recent Israeli army practice of beating and breaking bones in the effort to putdown the Arab uprising called the *intifada* was condemned by many Jews both in Israel and in the Diaspora as "un-Jewish." Some years ago in Jerusalem I was the unwilling witness of a brutal street fight between two Jews. "Un-Jewish!" said another witness, an Israeli who claimed to be "nonreligious" and to reject the *shtetl* image of the Jew, but who saw the conduct of the two street brawlers as contrary to all Jewish norms.[39]

The pejorative "un-Christian" is a frequently heard term. It is usually applied to attitudes of harshness and failure to forgive and to actions that betray uncharitableness. The terms overlap. There are those who would view bullfighting as "un-Christian," whereas Jewish tradition regards the unwillingness to forgive as "un-Jewish."[40]

The entire month of *Elul* is given over to reconciliation "between a person and another human being." The obligation to seek forgiveness from our fellows is matched by the obligation to forgive, and anyone who withholds forgiveness when it is sincerely sought is regarded as "cruel."[41]

The value terms that characterize Jewish distinctiveness help shape the social values of the group. They are not "otiose like the whistle on a locomotive," as someone has said. Rather, they are crucially determinative. This is a fact evident even to the most committed empirical-naturalists. Ernest Nagel writes that

> *only if one abandons all normal canons of evidence and ignores well-established empirical findings, can one deny that the beliefs men hold, or the reasons men advance for what they do and profess, often are crucial determining factors in historical processes.*[42]

Social values are established or are overturned by group practice. The initial "commands" or motivating principles may be enunciated by a great teacher, a prophet, or even a demagogue. They become more than casual or inefficacious when they are adopted in practical application by the group. The dark side of this process is exemplified by the chain of development from Nietzsche's *umwerthung des alle werthe*, "the overturning of all values," to the effect of Hitler's magnetic oratory and the collective evil of Nazism.[43]

The conflict between this "dark side" and the social values of Judaism manifested in Hitler's hatred of all things Jewish testifies to the necessary role of those very values in the effort to establish God's dominion on earth.

3
Are All Created Equal?

The insistence that all human beings are "neighbors," as Leo Baeck interprets the tradition, and the rabbinic belief that all are created in the image of God and that a portion of the divine presence is found in each person, imply a kind of equality of humankind. This is given vivid expression in the rabbinic conception of the common origin of all humanity. "Why was Adam created single?" the Talmud asks. "This is to teach us," the rabbis answer, "that no one may claim ancestry superior to that of any other individual."[1] Further, every individual is precious and "Anyone who destroys a single person is regarded as if he had destroyed the entire world, while anyone who saves a single person is regarded as if he had saved the entire world."[2]

In the phrase "a kind of equality," however, lies the beginning of the effort to hedge the concept of equality. We may well ask "what is this business of equality?" It has never existed, never been achieved.[3] The founders of the American republic held it to be "self-evident, that all men are created equal." Some limitation is needed before we can confidently mouth the words of the immortal Declaration of Independence. In factual terms, it just isn't so. In reality, we are born with built-in inequalities: we have differing endowments in the realm of intelligence, in physical capacities, and in a variety of genetic advantages and disadvantages.

The word "equality" is less problematic when it is used to connote equality before God—a statement of faith—or equality before the law—a principle and a goal. In the words of the Declaration, we are endowed with "unalienable rights," which should mean equality of opportunity. Everyone, regardless of the inequalities of birth endowment, should be free to "pursue happiness," free to realize in a lifetime the fulfillment of his or her potentialities.

Closely allied is the Kantian view of equality that all are free "moral agents." James Martin relates this concept to Kant's assertion of "an irreducible distinction between facts and values." This distinction holds

> in the realm of morality, between "is" and "ought." The rationale of practice—of "practical reason"— cannot be derived from the rationale of knowledge—of "pure reason." The world of conduct and its duties demands its own analysis, or "critique". . . The referent of the religious concept, "God," Kant had said, cannot be established as an implication of factual experience. But in the basic "given" of the analysis of moral judgments—the "categorical imperative" to recognize the equality of all men *as* moral aqents [my emphasis] . . . there is implied a giver and a guarantor of moral law. The existence of God, problematic in terms of "pure reason" alone, is a "necessary postulate" of "practical reason."[4]

Normative Jewish thought goes a step further. We may not, in terms of our differences in innate endowments, be equally valued. Human equality in most other senses is not a given, but a goal. And despite the rhetoric of democracy, we are a very long way from its realization.

Securing the "unalienable rights" that flow from that equality is the task of government. This is the specific conclusion of the first sentence of the American Declaration of Independence. Yet even in the time of its issuance and for more than three-quarters of a century longer, slavery was tolerated in the colonies. The *egalité* of the French revolution was first demonstrated by the guillotine, which did not discriminate between aristocrat and bourgeois. The Marxist quest for a classless society did not see a nation of privilege and the conquest of deprivation in the Soviet Union. The homeless on American streets, persons with mental illness prematurely discharged from psychiatric hospitals, people with disabilities, and the victims of prejudice—all are evidence that equality as a social value has thus far eluded even those who with good will have sought to establish it.

It was the high value they accorded the concept of human equality that led the prophets of Israel—especially the great preachers of social justice in the eighth century B.C.E.—to concern themselves with the insistent and perennial needs of the deprived and dispossessed levels of society. "The commiserated classes," Abraham Cronbach called them: the poor, the stranger or alien sojourner, the widow, the orphan. But the prophetic response was something more than commiseration or compassion. The prophets thundered against the unrighteousness of situations that brought exploitation and misery upon the poor and dispossessed, and against the smug and self-satisfied among the exploiters. "Woe to those who join house to house and lay field to field," driving the debt-ridden peasants into landlessness and exclusion from the goods of society—God's goods, they held.[5] Indeed, the rich landowners had themselves laid the burden of debt upon the poor. They sold the needy into servitude in requital for a minuscule sum equivalent to the price of a pair of straw sandals. Meanwhile they lay on "couches of ivory" and drank wine in bowls, ignoring the plight of the oppressed, for which they themselves were responsible.[6]

So great is the prophets' indignation that they assign to the dispossessed a special place in God's love: they are God's people. Isaiah boldly affirms this: "'What mean you that you crush My people and grind the face of the poor,' says the Lord of Hosts." Their derogation of ritual and ceremony is founded on the incongruity of the gap between prayer and righteous actions. "Who has required you to trample my courts?"—to come in such numbers to festival ceremonies in the Temple. Piety is fraud and hypocrisy if it does not lead to righteous conduct. God, says Isaiah, is unable to put up with the combination of evildoing and worship. And a great prophetic voice we have already quoted—probably that of a member of a "school of Isaiah"—eloquently defines true worship. It is not fasting and outward show but feeding the hungry and clothing the naked and sheltering the homeless.[7]

The prophetic voice was giving expression to something much more compelling than a mere attitude or ethical judgment. It was God's will, they taught, that all the inhabitants of God's world should share equally in its treasures. "The earth is the Lord's and the fullness thereof . . ."[8] Their insistence on this conviction and their effective teaching were what produced a startlingly bold scheme for the redistribution of wealth through a unique institution. It was an institution whose purposes were probably never realized in practice. The setting of the times did not permit it, but it remains a glorious statement of intent. That institution was the Jubilee.

The Hebrew word that has found a place in American Christendom as "Jubilee" and that was a symbol of hope in the antebellum spirituals of blacks in slavery is *yovel*. This term is connected with the ram's horn, the *shofar* that is to proclaim "liberty throughout the land to all its inhabitants" on the Day of Atonement of the fiftieth year.[9] Not only shall slaves go free, but all are to return to their own patrimonies, to the lands that were the possessions of their ancestors. In other words, everyone is to go back to square one. That the concept and the statute are late is indicated by their connection with the Day of Atonement, which itself was a late observance. It was visionary and in all likelihood unenforceable. The year of Jubilee was not observed after the exile and possibly not before it, but it is probably history's earliest socially motivated land reform proposal. It clearly embodies the prophetic commitment to human equality. There shall be no difference in the instructions given with respect to the native-born and the instructions with respect to the alien who dwells with you, the Torah commands (Exod. 12:49). As for those who have "joined themselves to the Lord" and have accepted the covenant, and observe the Sabbath, they will be brought to the mountain on which God's presence rests and rejoice in the Temple, "for My house shall be called a house of prayer for all peoples."[10]

The rabbis whose thought is represented in the oral tradition —the colloquies, the dialogues, the debates in the Talmud—were heirs of the prophets in more ways than are generally recognized. There were, it is true, major differences in their social setting and situation—especially after the destruction in 70 C.E. Unlike the prophets, they were not preachers. They were scholars and teachers, and their words are preserved in a setting of academic discussion the proceedings of which were memorized and then noted down as "Talmud." The prophets were individuals endowed with talent in rhetoric and oratory. Their deeply held convictions, ascribed to a divine voice that, they held, spoke through them, were expressed in vivid poetic form. But although they were individuals with sharply defined and diverse personalities, their preaching reflected a set of social values so common to all of them that it is possible to speak of a "prophetic movement."

The main line of rabbinic thinking was governed by those values: the supreme place of compassion, justice as a primary need but subsidiary to compassion, the deep concern for natural or human rights, and that universalism that saw all human beings as equally the children of the one God.[11] Out of those values grew that openness and receptivity to all opinions in free discourse that, paradoxically, led the rabbis to entertain and to record those opinions that veered away from the norm—even in some cases to the point of denying it. The aphorisms of the sages, collected in the work popularly named *Pirkay Avot,* or "Chapters of the Fathers," provide a convenient place for testing these descriptive statements. A treasury of practical wisdom as well as of ethical injunctions, this collection seems at the outset to be couched in universal terms and to be directed to *kol ha-b'riyot,* all of God's human creatures. Indeed, it begins with the affirmation by Simon the Just[12] that one of the three pillars on which the world rests is *g'milut ḥasadim,* voluntary acts of loving kindness. The tradition that follows, after one additional sage whose name was Antigonos,[13] was carried forward by the *zugot,* pairs of scholars thought to have been the presiding officers of the Council of Sages. A member of the first pair, Yose ben Yoḥanan of Jerusalem, is quoted as saying, "Let your home be open wide and let the poor be members of your household . . ." —something more than mere hospitality, for it reflects the attitude toward the needy that was found in the prophets.[14]

The chapter continues with an injunction to give everyone *(kol ha-adam)* "the benefit of the doubt" by judging them in "the scale of merit"—tipping the balance in their favor.[15] It comes to a climax in the frequently quoted statement of Hillel the Elder, an older contemporary of Jesus, "paired" with Shammai, who was portrayed (by the school of Hillel!) as the opposite of Hillel in temperament and viewpoint. Hillel's statement is an injunction to "love peace and pursue peace"—to love one's fellow creatures *(b'riyot)* and to bring them near to the Torah.[16] Nor is Shammai's contribution as rigid and particularistic as the Hillelites would have us believe, for he advises us to receive every person *(kol ha-adam)* with a cheerful countenance.[17]

Could it be that the stereotype of the ingratiating smile and the seeming subservience of the ghetto or *shtetl* Jew bears some relationship to Shammai's advice? One reason that it may not be too farfetched to think so lies in the fact that every Jew who attended or attends synagogue services regularly (and that meant the entire organic community with very few exceptions) was and is familiar with *Pirkay Avot* ("The Chapters of the Fathers"). It is the one tractate of the Talmud that is printed in its entirety, frequently accompanied by the major commentaries, in the *siddur*, the order of services or prayer book for daily and Sabbath worship. One *perek*, or chapter, is customarily read every Sabbath from Passover to Shavu'ot, the Feast of Weeks (Pentecost), and in some communities from Passover to Rosh Hashana, the religious New Year.

Shammai's word, it must be noted, continues the universalistic temper of *Avot* by its inclusiveness. Receiving every person cheerfully means aliens and strangers and, indeed, even one's enemies.[18] This is in accord with the frequent biblical references to a conciliatory approach to one's enemies, from the injunction to help raise up the fallen animal of the one who hates you to the word of the book of Proverbs that if your enemy is hungry you must give him bread to eat—not so that you may be rewarded, says the ingenious rabbinic interpretation,[19] but in order to make peace between you.

In the same spirit, Hillel does a reformulation of the biblical warning "not to follow a multitude into going astray." Hillel offers a positive version: "In the place where there are no men, strive to be a man."[20] The words *anashim* and *ish*—men and man—are in this context terms of approbation.[21] This is akin to the Yiddish use of the word *mentsch*. *Mentschlichkeit* is a state of being that includes decency, a positive stance, a courageous firmness in the right. "Be a *mentsch!*" is an injunction that can be addressed to any person and to either sex.

The insistence on a humanity that supersedes ethnic or national divisions is found again in the same chapter, where Rabbi Yehosh'ua proclaims that hatred of any of God's human creatures is a great enough sin in itself to "remove from the world" anyone who commits it.

The term *b'riyot*, so frequently used in *Avot*, means "creatures," and the verb *bara* usually has God as its subject and refers not to "all creatures great and small" but to human beings. This is true of the selections cited. It appears again in an aphorism ascribed to Rabbi Ḥanina ben Dosa:

"Anyone from whom the spirit of *b'riyot* [fellow humans] derives satisfaction, the spirit of the Omnipresent will [also] derive satisfaction."²³

The word "man" *(adam)* in its generic sense—man or woman, or any person—is used synonymously with *b'riyot*, as in Akiba's frequently quoted statement, "Beloved is Man in that he was created in the image [of God]; and he is additionally beloved in that it was made known to him that he was created in the image, as it is said, 'for in the image of God, He made Man.'"²⁴

The equality here portrayed is equality of opportunity to be righteous, to give evidence of those values that are the will of God.

The sages underline this thought as derived from the biblical pronouncement "Ye shall keep My statutes and My ordinances which if a man do, he shall *live* by them" by pointing to the fact that the verse cited does not say "which if a priest or a Levite or an Israelite do" but rather says "which if a man [person] do." Thus, they conclude, even "a pagan who studies Torah is equal to a high priest."²⁵ This equality of opportunity to achieve righteousness applies to other-worldly salvation as well, as indicated by the affirmation that "the righteous of the nations will have a portion in the world to come."²⁶ Such achievements of righteousness may be occasional or sporadic, but they are deemed to occur frequently enough to testify to the image of the Divine in all persons. This is seen in the word of Ben Azzai, who cautions us against despising or holding in contempt any human being *(kol adam)*, "for there is no human being who does not have his hour."²⁷ The popular proverb paraphrasing Hamlet's exit line in Act V, Scene I, "every dog has his day," is anticipated here in a less harsh form, for to have one's "hour" would seem to connote spiritual achievement rather than material or physical success. This nuance appears and is confirmed in the saying of Rabbi Levi ben Yosef cited earlier: "If you show contempt for your fellow-human, know who it is for whom you are showing contempt: your Father in Heaven—for in the image of God, He made Man."

It would overburden this presentation were we to offer citations to demonstrate the continuity and hence normative quality of this line of thought through Jewish history to the present day.[28] Leo Baeck, whom we quoted at the beginning of this chapter, further clarifies the meaning of love of neighbor by referring to the rabbinic sage who as previously noted, divided the verse into its two halves: *V'ahavta l're-echa ka-mocha,* "Love your neighbor as yourself," may be rendered *V'ahavta l're-echa,* "Love your neighbor" and *ka-mocha,* "he is just like you."

Abraham Geiger, an outstanding nineteenth-century Jewish thinker, declares, on the basis of the normative tradition, that the "whole human race" is "endowed with equal rights."[29] Far ahead of his time, and on the foundation of this heritage, Emil G. Hirsch of Chicago, the fiery progressive Jewish preacher, declared in 1911, at an international gathering:

> *We dispute that there is a man in the world who by reason of his colour, of his appearance, or of his descent has lost the power of valuing himself morally and of remaining true to his moral dignity. Consequently, we oppose racial hatred with all our might.*[30]

Hirsch's affirmation, in full consonance with the spirit of the normative Jewish tradition, parallels, *mutatis mutandis,* the outburst of a sage of the second century: "I call heaven and earth to witness that the holy spirit rests upon every person—non-Jew or Jew, man or woman, manservant or maid-servant, according to the measure of his deeds."[31]

This affirmation of human equality in the sense of human rights engages the active concern of Jews to this day. We shall have more to say about this in what follows.

4

Value Conflicts in Jewish Thought

We have mentioned the fact that there are polar opinions among the sages in rabbinic literature just as there are diverse and frequently conflicting ideas in Scripture. Indeed, the propensity of the rabbis is to seize both horns of every dilemma and force them together. This is what Martin Buber called "unity of the contraries."[1] Philosophical tradition preserves the term *coincidentia oppositorum*, associating it with the fifteenth-century thinker and prelate Nicholas Cusanus, who used it to describe what he saw as the identity of the individual with the universal, the finite with the infinite.[2]

One prime example of the clash of rabbinical opinions is found in the sages' discussions of capital punishment. Capital punishment is presented in matter-of-fact fashion in Scripture. The Bible prescribes various forms of execution for various offenses. How can this be reconciled with Judaism's affirmation of the supreme sanctity of life and the vaunted emphasis on the high value of compassion?

Here, as elsewhere in dealing with the harshness or violence of biblical material, the rabbis looked for loopholes. If the Bible required the death penalty, then the rabbinic sense of human dignity and the traditional abhorrence of inflicting pain had to motivate them to remove the cruelty of stoning, burning, beheading, or strangulation—the four biblical forms of execution.

They did this by making more and more stringent the rules of evidence and making it more and more difficult for courts to pronounce the death sentence.[3] Hence, even in Second Temple times, capital punishment became more and more rare, and the Pharisees eliminated it almost altogether.

The rarity of biblical executions in rabbinic times is testified to in an exchange between Rabbi Eleazar ben Zadok and his colleagues.[4] Rabbi Eleazar said that he had personally been eyewitness to the burning of the adulterous daughter of a priest. His fellow rabbis responded by saying that if that was so, the court was either ignorant or Sadducean.

Even more significant is the discussion in the next tractate of the Mishnah that anticipates by centuries modern debate on the subject. Rabbi Akiba and Rabbi Tarfon would have banned capital punishment entirely, whereas Rabban Shim'on ben Gamaliel saw it as a social necessity, a deterrent to capital crime. The entire discussion in the Talmud shows rabbinic distaste for the death penalty, because the *halacha* hedges it about with the aforesaid restrictions as to evidence and by the affirmative advantage given to acquittal.[5] The climax of the debate occurs when the rabbis offer the opinion that any Sanhedrin that sentenced one individual to death in any seven-year period would be known as *"havlanit"*—a destructive or reckless Sanhedrin. Rabbi Eleazar ben Azariah interjected, "Even once in seventy years!"—whereupon Rabbi Akiba and Rabbi Tarfon declared that if they had been members of the Sanhedrin, no one would ever have been executed. This statement drew from Rabban Shim'on ben Gamaliel, president of the academy, a descendant of Hillel, and a person of great rabbinic authority, the retort that (if this had been the case) "murderers would have increased in the land."[6] This exchange of conflicting opinions is interesting in that it sheds light on the homely character of talmudic discussion. It is opinion only: there was no vote and there need not have been any decision. The entire question was moot—the rabbinic courts had no authority to inflict capital punishment. But the value conflict is evident: which, in this context, is the more powerful motivating value—the sanctity of the individual life, or the putative protection of the community against capital crime?

There is a similar dilemma with respect to the matter of abortion—that is, abortion in the sense of deliberately induced termination of pregnancy. Unlike the matter of capital punishment, there is no direct basis in Scripture for rabbinic discussion of this problem.[7]

The rabbis are guided by three principles. One is the fact that Jewish tradition shows great respect for the physical body, influencing its decisions with respect to autopsy and other actions characterized as defilements, as well as with respect to abortion. Second, a fetus is not considered a person but is part of the mother [8]—a *nefesh*[9] is discerned only after birth, although this conclusion is not invoked in relating to the moral questions surrounding abortion. The fetus is not a *nefesh*, but it is "potential life," and is to be treated as such. The question of abortion after rape requires compassionate decision making. Here the casuistry or situational ethic of the rabbis comes into play. And third, the principle of protecting what is pursued *(nirdaf)* from the pursuer *(rodef)* is upheld. If the life of a pregnant woman is threatened by an abnormal development, then she is the pursued and the fetus is the pursuer and may be destroyed even up to term.[10]

The rabbinic authorities, for the most part, reject any analogy between rules concerning abortion and rules concerning contraception. Some contraceptive devices such as tampons and shields are definitely permitted and some modern orthodox *responsa* permit use of birth-control pills. What is forbidden is interference with the "proper" emission of the sperm—the biblical sin of Onan known in rabbinic Hebrew as *hash-ḥatat zera*, literally "destroying seed."[11]

It should be remarked that the very first *Mitzvah* in the Bible is the command to "Be fruitful and multiply and fill the earth." The value of large families frequently conflicts with the value concern for health and for life itself (even "mental anguish" that threatens life[12]), and the sometimes searing decision—not only in respect to abortion—of *which* life has priority when only one can be saved.

Here intent becomes important. Neither contraception nor abortion should be undertaken for convenience alone, financial or otherwise. The tradition, therefore, does not endorse unlimited freedom of choice, despite the fact that many progressive rabbis do so in regard to legal freedom. Responsibility to society, to the father as well as to the mother, and to safeguarding against self-pollution or ignoble motives must also be considered.

The abiding difference between Catholic doctrine on abortion and the Jewish tradition hinges on the question of ensoulment—but that subject is not only highly complex; it is also not immediately germane to our discussion of value conflict.[13]

Questions of this sort arise in all significant decision making, both in ancient literature and in modern life. The rabbinic tradition dramatizes this fact of value conflict by imagining quaintly that even God faces this problem, "if one might even suppose" such an eventuality. They picture God as bending the truth a little in order to preserve domestic peace. Sara behind the tent door hears the prophecy that she will bear a child and laughs because she is old—ninety years old—and she has "passed the manner of women." So Sara laughs and says, "At my age? . . . And my husband is old, too!" But in the next verse, as Bar Kappara emphasizes in a Midrash, God is reported as telling Abraham that Sara has said *she* is too old to have a child. God neglects saying anything about her having said that her husband was too old![14]

The "white lie" is thus given the highest endorsement. Elsewhere we read that because it is customary at a wedding to greet the bride with words praising her beauty, saying "O beautiful bride," the disciples of Hillel would say it even if the bride was seen as ugly, subordinating truth to the demand that one shall not humiliate a fellow human being in public—and, in any case, all brides *are* beautiful.[15]

The complexities that mark the area of economic life even in the relatively simple forms of organization found in the Bible are a fertile field for value conflicts. A biblical law founded in the best of intentions often threatens to harm those it was meant to help. An instance of this is the institution of *sh'mita*, the release of all debts in the seventh—or sabbatical—year.[16] The purpose of the sabbatical year, it must be noted, was "that the poor may eat"—the fields were to lie fallow and the poor were permitted to come and take whatever grew of itself. The cancellation of debts was also, obviously, for the benefit of the poor. But what the Deuteronomist either anticipated or observed came to pass. "Beware," says the text, "that there be not a thought in your wicked heart, saying, 'The seventh year, the year of release, is at hand,' and your eye is evil against your poor brother and you give him nothing . . ."[17] This insight into human nature was confirmed in the event. The unwillingness to lend money in the sixth year threatened the entire economic structure, not just the poor alone. A way had to be found to deal with the problem without either eliminating the institution of the sabbatical year and its benevolent purpose or placing a burden on the lender or the individual who needed to borrow. That way was found by Hillel the Elder.[18] His device was labeled with the Greek term *prosbul*, which means an order of the court. The debt at the time the loan had been made was placed under the jurisdiction of the *bet din*, the court of law, so that when the sabbatical year had concluded the lender might be paid.[19]

In the area of business ethics, the principle of *tsedek*—equity—is a controlling value. Just weights and measures calling for the utmost exactitude are ordained in the Torah.[20] There are, however, situations in which exactitude is not enough. In those situations a truly ethical response may call for generosity or compassion. What developed in response to this was a set of responses called *Mishnat Ḥasidim*, regulations for those who are especially pious, who are governed by *ḥesed*, loving kindness.[21] These will act *Lifnim mi-shurat ha-din* ("within the line of the law"). They will not take advantage of everything that is permitted to them but will do more than is required.[22]

The Talmud tells a story that illustrates the preferred response to a conflict between the halachic system and what we may call "higher" values. Rabba ben bar Ḥana was a vintner as well as a scholar *(talmid ḥacham)*. One day two of his employees who were carrying a cask of wine were negligent and dropped it, spilling its contents. Regarding himself as legally entitled to compensation, Rabba ben bar Ḥana withheld their wages and took their cloaks in pledge for the damages owed to him. The laborers took their case to Rab, the head of the academy, and complained that with Rabba having taken their cloaks they would have no covering against the chill of the night. Rab found for them and said to Rabba, "Give them back their cloaks." "Is this the law?" asked Rabba. "Yes," said Rab, "for it is written, 'that you may walk in the way of good men'"—so Rabba gave them back their cloaks. But the two porters persisted in their complaint. "He has withheld our wages. Must we go hungry? We'll not have the wherewithal to purchase food." And Rab said, "Pay them their wages." Said Rabba, "Is this the law?" "Yes," said Rab, "for it is also written, 'that you shall keep the paths of the righteous.'" So Rabba paid them their wages.[23]

What is extraordinary and revealing of the rabbinic stance in this story is that Rab—a great halachic authority —went beyond legalism and appealed to an abstract general idea of "righteousness," motivated by a concern for simple, human need. More so, he could have cited as authority for his decision the injunction in the Torah, "If you take your fellow's garment in pledge, you must return it before the sun goes down. It is his only covering in which he may lie down. It may be that he will cry to Me and I shall hear him—for I am compassionate."[24]

All these conflicts dissolve in their confrontation with that which is normatively and possibly unchallengeably the supreme value—namely, the sanctity of life. This is so despite the agonizing problem of capital punishment as described earlier in this chapter: *Pikuaḥ nefesh*—the saving of life overrides all of the commandments of the Torah.[25]

It can be said, therefore, that Jesus was in the mainstream of the oral Torah when, healing on the Sabbath, he declared "The Sabbath was made for man—not man for the Sabbath."[26] Indeed, this dictum paraphrases a rabbinic dictum that makes the same affirmation. Found in an early Midrash, it reads "The Sabbath was handed over to you; you were not handed over to the Sabbath."[27] Or again, in the same passage, "Let one Sabbath be profaned in order that (by doing so) you may observe many Sabbaths." "The commandments were given to you so that you should live by them," not that you should die because of them, says another Midrash.[28]

The *halacha* is casuistic or, to use a modern term, "situational." Every case must stand "on its own legs" and be decided on its merits. However, every decision is made in the light of overarching values to which attention must be given. An interesting example cited earlier occurs in a halachic discussion about the plight of an individual who is half-slave and half-free. Evidently, half his freedom has been purchased either by himself or by a benefactor. The discussion concerns his work obligations. The school of Hillel rules that he should work half-time for his owner and half-time for himself. But, interestingly, the school of Shammai, reputed to be more rigid, is in this instance more alert to the ethical values in the situation. You cannot leave him half-slave and half-free, they insist. In that situation, he would never be able to marry—as a slave he cannot marry a free person and as a freeman he cannot marry a slave.

"The world was not made to be a waste," the Shammaites declare. You must buy out the rest of his freedom so that he may fulfill the *mitzva* to "be fruitful and multiply." And the Hillelites agree! Therefore, the decision is according to the view of the school of Shammai. The basis of the decision is not a citation from the Torah. Rather, it is something that must be done *mip'ne tikkun ha'olam*, because of the need to mend or improve the world.[29]

The concern that the Shammaites show for the human needs of the slave and that the Hillelites are unable to resist, is the rabbinic view that is part of their self-image and the self-image of the Jew, that Jews are *Raḥmanim b'ne raḥmanim*—the compassionate children of compassionate parents. When a biblical ordinance or expression offended this rabbinic stance, they boldly sought the means to overturn it or to void it. Two specific instances of this rabbinic response are the case of the stubborn and rebellious son and the woman accused of adultery.[30]

Among the harsh decrees involving capital punishment in the Torah, the decree against an allegedly incorrigible son goes too far. To condemn a person to death on the say-so of his parents violates human sensibilities and stands in contradiction to commands imbued with mercy and love. Scripture prescribes that the parents shall take their son to the judges and say, "He will not obey our voice," he is stubborn, "a glutton and a drunkard," and they can do nothing with him. Whereupon, on the judges' decree, he is taken out and stoned to death. How do the rabbis deal with this? They fasten on the words "our voice" in the text and say the parents must speak with absolute simultaneity as with one voice and in the same pitch. The near impossibility of this leads to the rabbis' conclusion that the case of the stubborn and rebellious son never arose, never existed. The law was void.[31]

The same technique is used by the rabbis in the case of the red heifer, the paradoxical problem that "gave Satan an opening." The ashes that are used to purify are also the source of impurity. But the Torah says you must take a red heifer "without blemish"—meaning not even one white hair. Where can one find such a heifer? Not one in a million! "These laws were given to us only that we might study them and receive our reward." The value conflict between a pious respect for Scripture and a commitment to rationality as well as to justice is thus solved—surgically.[32]

In the case of the woman suspected of adultery, the Torah prescribes a trial that smacks of magic and superstition. She is required to drink a concoction of bitter waters and if its effect is to cause her belly to swell, she is held guilty of adultery. The rabbinic response to this was simply to void the entire procedure: "When adulterers multiplied, they voided the bitter water test and Rabbi Yoḥanan ben Zakkai was the one who voided it."[33]

The rabbinic resort to exegetical techniques to overturn or void biblical propositions that conflict with their values is also displayed in the way in which they deal with the acceptance and even seeming exaltation of violence in Scripture. We shall look into this when later we discuss the high value that Jewish thought accords to nonviolence.

The possibility of value conflict becomes especially evident, as we have already suggested, in matters of business ethics. Roman law comes down on the side of the vendor with its doctrine of *caveat emptor*—"let the buyer beware." In the Levant, bargaining is so customary that the vendor in a folk market is disappointed if a buyer accepts the vendor's first price quotation.

The quaint tale of Abraham's bargaining with the "children of Ḥeth" for the cave of Machpela in Ḥebron offers an insight into Middle Eastern manners in matters of trade.[34] Ephron the Hittite's opening gambit is to tell Abraham that he may have the land as a gift. When Abraham protests that he wishes to pay, Ephron names the price by saying that the land is worth only four hundred shekels of silver and then says, "What is that between you and me? Take it and bury your dead." In this instance

Abraham hears, and wanting the cave and the land as a "sure possession" with full and enduring legal title, he meets Ephron's price and weighs out the silver in the presence of witnesses in the city gate of Hebron. In this byplay there is no mention of market value. The special circumstances make it an atypical instance of purchase without bargaining.

Value conflict is potential, however, because the rules intended to protect traders against inequities must not be allowed, it was thought, to interfere with commerce and thus with the economic health of the community, as was already indicated in our discussion of the sabbatical year.

Unlike the Roman response, Jewish law holds both buyer and seller responsible to act in accord with the principle of *tsedek*—equity. An example of the responsibility of the vendor is found in the story of a sage named Rabbi Safra who had an article to sell. A man came and offered to buy it, naming a price, but Rabbi Safra was engaged in prayer and therefore did not answer because it was not proper to interrupt his prayer in order to do so. The prospective buyer thought that the rabbi did not answer because the price he had offered was too low and so he raised his offer. But when Rabbi Safra finished praying he said, "You may have it for the price you first mentioned because I had intended to let you have it for that amount."[35]

The buyer has the responsibility not to pay less than what he or she knows the article to be worth and not to mislead the seller by creating the impression of being interested in buying when he or she has no intention of doing so.[36] How easy it is to violate this principle. One finds a beautiful or valuable book in a junk shop and accepts the seller's price or even bargains with the seller to get the book for less when one knows it to be worth much more. Here there is a problem of determining monetary value. But to take advantage of the seller's ignorance of the actual worth of the item is *g'nevat da-at*, "stealing his mind."[37] Not only is it theft, but it is also a violation of the Torah command, "Thou shalt not place a stumbling-block before the blind."[38]

Business ethics in Jewish thought is directly affected by the concept of *kiddush ha-shem,* the protection so to speak of God's reputation. Contrary to popular opinion sparked by Jew-haters, it is far worse for a Jew to take advantage of a non-Jew than it is to take advantage of a fellow Jew. A Jew who cheats a Jew is guilty of fraud; a Jew who cheats a non-Jew not only is guilty of fraud but also has "profaned the name of God"—a *hillul hashem.*[39]

Philip Wylie embedded the ancient canard that a Jew may cheat a non-Jew in his book *Generation of Vipers,* where he states that the non-Jew is "fair game."[40] That this contention is libelous is testified to in *halachic* decisions, in anecdotes, and in what we know of general Jewish practices. The *halachic* Jew has acted with impressive faithfulness to the spirit of the biblical commands about "the stranger." Needless to say, there have always been sinners and cheats, from Second Isaiah's excoriation of those who pursue their business in the day of their fast[41] to the sharp practices and inside trading reported in our own day. The rabbinic dicta on business ethics are not mere "counsels of perfection," but rules to be followed in daily life. Leo Jung wrote:

> *The* pinkesim *[community records] spanning one and a half millennia of Jewish life in the ghettoes, provide the answer. The ordinances and regulations of the local* bet din *[rabbinic court] convey a true and full picture of how the Torah's individual and social ethics were translated into the behavior of the average Jew . . . a clear record of a consistent, dedicated, and on the whole eminently successful endeavor to keep Jews on the moral and spiritual heights of Judaism notwithstanding the innumerable intrusions by hostile clerics, governments, and local tyrants and the heavy burden of often hopeless poverty.*[42]

This responsiveness to values that exercise superiority over legal enactments emerges from unbiased study of how *halacha* was applied. It provided the most important tool for conflict resolution: casuistry. This means casuistry in the best sense—that is, openness to all the facets of each case, each problem. It is this characteristic of openness—the obligation to look at each case in all its facets and from every possible perspective—that informs the rabbinic tendency or, one might say, rabbinic technique of posing problems that elicit disagreements and then handling them in a manner that produces agreement.[43] The term "conflict resolution," which describes this kind of activity in contemporary thought, also describes a major goal of the rabbinic process of two thousand years ago. Biblical thought regards the effort to eliminate conflict as an especially demanding obligation, indeed often regarded as the greatest of all demands.[44] The word for it is *shalom*, which in this context means total well-being in interpersonal relations.

But as the rabbis held *shalom* to be a supreme objective, in a typical rabbinic paradox they affirmed that conflict is also good. Conflict is good if it is measured and conditioned by its intention. It is good, for instance, if it is a disagreement about how best to fulfill the divine will. "Every controversy which is for the sake of Heaven will endure"[45]—that is, it will produce a constructive result. Or it is good if it leads toward truth. "Debate or argument is useful because it establishes [or makes clear] the truth," said Rabbi Obadiah of Bertinoro.[46] The objective is to resolve the conflict and to raise the discussion to a new level.

The sages were not content to rely on verbal interplay alone. They devised structured procedures through which the settlement of conflict would be achieved in a manner that would make peace between the parties to the conflict. This was to supersede a resort to power or force, as represented by a court of law, resulting in an imposed decision with its residue of potential resentment in defeat and consequent continued hostility.[47]

The procedures were not haphazard. They were thoughtfully planned methods of bringing the conflicting parties to arbitration or, better yet, of effecting a compromise. The overriding value, we see again, is *shalom*.

There are two terms for the arbitral procedure. One is *bitsuah,* an etymologically difficult word, and the other is *pesharah,* the achievement of a compromise acceptable to both parties.[48] In talmudic usage, the two terms seem to coalesce and are used interchangeably. According to Rabbi Joshua ben Korha, settlement by *bitsuah* is a *mitzvah,* and this is the normative judgment.[49] A contrary opinion is expressed by Rabbi Eliezer ben Yose, who insisted "let the law cut through the mountain" because, in his view, judgment is the prerogative of God alone.[50] The clarifying word comes from Maimonides, who writes:

> *It is a* mitzvah *at the outset, to offer the contenders the option "Do you prefer* din *[legal judgment] or* pesharah *[compromise] to resolve your conflict?" If they choose* pesharah, *then they [the judicial authorities] effect* pesharah *between them. And every* bet din *[court] which always [seeks to] make use of* pesharah *is accounted praiseworthy.*[51]

A modern orthodox authority (Ha-rav Soloveitchik) explains why this interpretation is favored:

> Din *pits one party against the other . . . the law is administered with cold impartiality . . . one party emerges the victor; his case is vindicated. The plea of the other is denied. Discord and resentment persist even as the court docket is cleared and the case is closed. The legal issue has been resolved but human bitterness continues to fester.*
>
> *In* pesharah, *however, social harmony is the primary concern . . . the goal is not to be juridically astute but to be socially healing. The psychology of the contenders, their socio-economic status and values, as well as the general temper of society are the primary ingredients employed in the* pesharah *process . . . the final resolution of the conflict is a delicate and sensitive blending of both objective legal norms and subjective*

humanistic goals. For this reason, pesharah *is the preferred alternative.*[52]

Another reason that *pesharah* is preferred is that legal procedures usually require the litigants to place themselves under oath. *Pesharah* obviates that need. This is of more than passing importance because the tradition, and popular attitude, are wary regarding oaths that are understood to have an awesome irrevocability.[53] Hence the annual disclaimer in the *Kol Nidre* (All Vows) on the eve of the Day of Atonement and the pious Jew's habit of accompanying even the most innocuous statements of intention with the phrase *b'li neder*, meaning "I am not taking an oath that I'll fulfill it."

The often-quoted verse "Justice, justice shalt thou pursue" is held relevant here by some commentators. The word "justice" is repeated, they say, because the first is for *din* whereas the second is for *pesharah*. Others relate the entire verse to compromise, which is considered to be marked by a twofold need for justice, in that the burden of impartial care and fine-tuned analysis rests entirely on the arbitrator.[54]

It is of special interest to our inquiry to note that Joshua ben Korḥa found scriptural authority for his belief that *bitsuah* is a *mitzvah* in the verse "Execute the judgment of truth and peace in your gates," interpreting it to mean that judgment in a dispute must be attended by both truth and *shalom*.[55] The sages reflect further on this, adding "where there is [strict] justice [*mishpat*] there is no peace [*shalom*]. And where there is peace, there is no strict justice. But where do we find *mishpat* in which there is *shalom*? This is *bitsuah*."[56]

Commenting on this, Rabbi Soloveitchik echoes Martin Buber's "unity of the contraries." Soloveitchik writes:

> *In Aristotelian logic, there is a law of contradiction which states that a thesis and its antithesis cannot both be valid . . . if A is right, B must be wrong . . . the* halachah, *however, believes that absolute right and wrong can be realized only in "heaven." In dealing*

with imperfect man we posit that no man is totally wrong or right . . .[57]

The more profound point toward which we are reaching here is that both *mishpat* and *shalom* are necessary and therefore must coexist. That this is a paradox is not a source of difficulty for the sages. Again and again, we come to see their predilection for paradox. The world of thought, like the physical world, presents itself with many facets, and the way in which we apprehend them is a matter of perspective. Seemingly contradictory propositions may signal a conflict of inadequately understood truths. Buber explored this idea when he offered a resolution of the seemingly unresolvable contradiction in a well-known aphorism of the great second-century teacher, Rabbi Akiba. Akiba taught "everything is foreseen and yet we are given freedom to choose".[58] Both determinism and free will are here affirmed in one sentence. How can both be correct? This is Buber's answer:

> *It is only when reality is turned into logic and A and non-A dare no longer dwell together, that we get determinisms and indeterminisms, a doctrine of predestination and a doctrine of freedom, each excluding the other. According to the logical conception of truth, only one of two contraries can be true, but in the reality of life as one lives it, they are inseparable . . . The person who makes a decision knows that his deciding is no self-delusion. The person who has acted knows that he was and is in the hand of God. The unity of the contraries is the mystery at the innermost core of the dialogue.*[59]

Akiba's polar contradiction, like all paradoxes, may be resolved by imaginative and creative analysis. On the other hand, it may forever challenge us to recognize the limitations of the human intellect. It can be an expression of intellectual humility.

We may also conclude that the rabbinic responses to

the major antinomies of life reflect the tensions felt by human beings in everyday relationships: parent and child, husband and wife, worker and co-worker, employer and employee. By a response of projection, we ascribe the same tensions to the divine. Is God torn between a will to justice and deep compassion? What does a concerned parent feel when he or she sees a child slipping into some destructive pattern: drug abuse, alcoholism, or careless promiscuity? Modern psychologists often advise firmness. They call it "tough love" and the very phrase is an oxymoron. Can one be firm and at the same time loving and supportive? Absence of firmness in a parent brings consequent dependence and weakness in the child. Tough love would look ahead—beyond the crisis of the moment—in order to create self-sufficiency, the ability in the child to stand on his or her own feet.

These existential tensions—both the personal and the universal—are confronted by the rabbinic tradition. Normative Jewish thought rejects the "either-or" response and opts for the "both-and." Both sides of the apparent contradictions that mark the classical dualisms are embraced, bringing the searchers closer to the whole truth than could be grasped by one-sided consistency. Justice and mercy coexist, freedom and determination are affirmed, God is both "Wholly Other" and intimately present.

The tradition overcomes the dualisms or antinomies of religion through its openness to the rich variety of possibilities life offers and through its recognitions of the complexity and ultimate mystery that lie behind and beyond what we are able to perceive. It is this process that applies to the seemingly contradictory ideal of justice and mercy. They are value terms invoked in decision making, and one or the other, it could be held, must govern our choices. But in Jewish thought, those overarching values that condition the preference for *pesharah*—both justice and mercy (*mishpat* or *din*—the right conclusions—as opposed to *raḥamim*—compassionate love) are terms that point to supreme directives. God is represented in the Midrash, when challenged by Abraham, as "holding both ends of the line" and being unwilling to relinquish either—in other words, justice and mercy *can* coexist in the same context.

Leo Jung called this kind of affirmation of both poles of a seeming contradiction "tsedekism." *Tsedek* means equity, that which is correct, and is the root of the word *ts'daka*. *Tsedek*, says Jung, has a double meaning:

> *It should be translated as both justice and kindness . . . Nothing must interfere with the just processes of the law . . . (the law must pierce the mountain) but, on the other hand, the judge who is the representative of the God of justice and love must always be conscious of the difference between standard and application. Naked justice, the literal application of the law, is to be avoided. This requires righteous casuistry, a casuistry that ensures that the special conditions of each case are fully considered. The court of justice and kindness must endeavor to adjust some of the injustices of life; it must especially in borderline cases give the benefit of the doubt to the underdog. . . . The judge must even balance out what might favor those who are financially, socially, or otherwise advantaged. In Jewish law, the protection of the weaker is not a matter of mercy but of applied justice. Therefore, whenever the benefit of doubt is to be granted, the poor should be favored over the rich, the unprotected laborer over the employer, the woman over the man, the friendless alien over the well-established citizen.*[60]

The rabbis reached this same conclusion, and they did so through deliberate disregard of the clear meaning of the biblical text. This kind of deliberate emendation is exalted to its highest degree in a significant omission of two words in the great theophany of Exodus 34 when it is read at a most solemn moment in the worship services for the high holy days and the three pilgrim festivals. The passage in Scripture reads:

> *The Lord, The Lord God merciful and gracious, long-suffering with abundant loving kindness and truth,*

forgiving iniquity, transgression and sin—v'nakay lo y'nakey—*but by no means declaring the guilty to be innocent . . .*⁶¹

In the prayer book version, however, the two words *lo y'nakey* are omitted so that, making allowance for a grammatical lapse, it would read "forgiving iniquity, transgression and sin, and declaring innocent . . ."

This is either a kind of *absit omen*, an unwillingness to give an opening to the forces of evil, or a pious affirmation that it is God's nature to forgive. In this theophany, there are two names for God: The tetragrammaton, read *adonay*, and the word *el*. The customary view would hold that *el* stands for God's justice and *adonay* for God's mercy. Here, however, they are recited in a fervent declaration that God is forgiving and loving. In a quaint bit of imagery—a *kiv'yachol* ("if it could be imagined so")—God even prays. God prays that His attribute of mercy *(midat haraḥamim)* will overcome His attribute of justice *(midat ha-din)*.

Decision making in Jewish practice operates on two levels: the legal level, which "expresses the normal principle of mutuality and reciprocity"; and the moral level, where the concept of *kiddush ha-shem* makes for heightened ethical sensitivity. Leo Jung illustrates this thought with the example of the *halachic* determination regarding the return of lost property to a non-Jew. On the legal level, reciprocity requires a Jew to restore lost property only in countries where such restoration is enforced on all inhabitants. Where non-Jews, in accordance with local law and custom, operate on the basis of "finders keepers," Jews are not legally obliged to return lost property, either. But on the basis of *kiddush ha-shem*, taking advantage of a technicality or a legal escape stands "counter to the moral imperative of the Torah. The Jew must restore the lost property of his gentile neighbors."⁶²

Here we encounter the factor of the value perspective that accounts for much of the successful resolution of conflict present in the application of Jewish ethical convictions to practical affairs. Each case involving decision making obliges every person, judge, or layman to view the facts from every angle before subjecting them to a determination. The decision, however, must involve the inherited values: the perennial aspects of a value stance marked by openness, compassion, truth, and social concern.

5

From Rhetoric to Practice

To this point I have, for the most part, offered statements from the Jewish value heritage—"the tradition says this" and "the tradition says that." But to what extent do the doctrines we have quoted remain rhetoric, affirmative of value concepts, and to what extent do they impel those who recite them to fulfill them in action? The major emphasis of the value heritage has been on conduct. This is the effect of the central role that *mitzvah* plays in Jewish thought. The injunctions that are intended to guide action are not simply value concepts. They are divine demands that have exerted compelling power in ensuring the obedience of the *halachic* Jew. That power has been the foundation for the amazing faithfulness of the Jewish people through the ages to the *mitzvot* and to conduct fully responsive to the biblical "thou shalts" and "thou shalt nots" as interpreted by the rabbinic tradition. The frequent reiteration, in the rabbinic tradition itself, of the controlling importance of the application of the value concepts to real-life situations has preserved and supported that stance.

At the very outset of the tractate *Avot* (1:17) of the Mishnah, Rabban Shim'on ben Gamaliel, whom we have already described as an outstanding authority,[1] pronounces the judgment that the *ikkar*, the most important aspect of the rabbinic teaching, is not the exposition (*midrash*) of Torah, but actual conduct (*ma-aseh*) in response to it.

In another talmudic passage, we read of a discussion about which is greater—study or practice. According to Rabbi Tarfon, it was study; according to Rabbi Akiba, it was practice. But the consensus was that study is great when it leads to action.[2] When one says the *Sh'ma*,[3] one takes upon oneself the yoke of the dominion of Heaven. But that is not sufficient: one must also take upon oneself the yoke of the commandments (*mitzvot*).[4]

The view of Torah as dynamic in motivating an active response has been widely held in Jewish thought. For example, an important eleventh-century philosopher, Bachya ibn Pakuda, whose dominant concerns were prayer and study and the "purification of the soul," warns the pious not to shun contact with the rest of humanity in order to devote themselves to the salvation of their own souls; they should rather teach mankind and lead them to the worship of God [in order to] accept life in this world as a task.[5]

This emphasis on the primary role of conduct is also found in the New Testament. James, who may have been the brother of Jesus, argues that "Faith without works is dead," and in doing so stands squarely within the Hebrew pharisaic tradition.[6]

Rabbis, in pursuit of "ethical perfection in a united humanity," sought through law and enactment to develop the process of applying high ethical ideals to the specific problems of daily life in the real world, according to Jacob Lauterbach.[7] The conceiving of these ideals, he adds, was done by great minds—prophets, priests, and teachers. Their practical implications had to be developed later. It is in this second category that he places the rabbis and teachers of the *halachah*.

The distinction holds on one level, but on another it seems too sharp. The prophets were frequently activists: Amos' preaching at Beth El, for instance, put him in danger of his life. Isaiah led protest demonstrations in Jerusalem, and Jeremiah was arrested and persecuted for his public demonstrations and resistance to authority.[8]

The rabbis were successors in spirit to the prophets

but their situations were very different. They could not deal with "affairs of state," but they could affect the lives and the conduct of those whom they could teach, and to whom they could transmit their view of what it was that God required of them. And they rose, when it was demanded of them, to the point of martyrdom—that is, to the moral and ethical level of the prophets.

The action that was demanded by them in the name of God was not self-serving but on behalf of others. Religious duties, such as relief to the poor, ransoming the captives, dowering a poor bride, and the like, took precedence over other practical concerns. Maimonides makes this clear when he says that funds raised for the building of a synagogue may first be called upon to meet pressing human needs.[9]

If, then, social concerns are not to remain in the realm of rhetoric alone, they require some degree of *institutionalization*—some societal structure that will make possible their concrete application. Such forms are found in the social devices set forth in Leviticus and Deuteronomy. The prophets were most troubled by the twin problems of landlessness and poverty. Their eighth century (B.C.E.) preaching eventuated in the biblical legislation we associate with the Deuteronomist who enacted practical solutions a century later. They were simple devices adequate to a relatively simple society. One such provision was the requirement that a landed farmer refrain from harvesting his entire crop. He was to leave part of it—the corners (*peah*)—for the "poor and the needy."[10]

How large is a corner? The simplicity of this prescription is indicated by the fact that such a size is nowhere specified in Scripture—it provides a subject for necessary definition by the rabbis.[11] The same Levitical verses enjoin that the gleanings (*leket*), that which is dropped in the course of harvesting, are not to be picked up but are to be left for those who are without resources. This is not a voluntary act. It is the right of the deprived. Even that which is involuntarily left unharvested—that which is forgotten—

belongs to the poor (*shik'cha*).[12] There is also the liberal but undefined provision that you may go into a vineyard not your own and eat your fill, but you may not carry any of the fruit away with you in a vessel[13]—which may very well be an extension of the rule in Leviticus intended to keep the poor from going hungry. And finally, among the biblical devices for more equitable distribution of the earth's goods, there is the institution of tithing,[14] through which one-tenth of one's produce becomes the property of the Levite, the stranger, the widow, and the orphan. This provision finds further development in rabbinic and medieval regulations and is practiced by genuinely pious people—Christians, Jews, and others—to this day.[15]

When we turn from the biblical to the rabbinic enactments we find a greater adaptation to the urban setting as opposed to the rural and agricultural background that was appropriate to the biblical milieu. Provision was now made for *ts'daka* (almsgiving) in the form of monetary gifts or gifts in kind. We are told that in the Temple in Jerusalem there were two special chambers: one was the "chamber of the silent," to which the pious might bring their gifts for the poor and deposit them anonymously, and from which the poor with equal anonymity might take for their needs.[16] The role of being a *matan b'seter*—one who gives secretly—was praised in Jewish thought as "greater than Moses our teacher."[17] The other chamber was for utensils and other household goods that were distributed every thirty days, and although the Temple seems to have had first claim, some sources indicate that it functioned as a kind of thrift shop in which the poor did not have to pay.

The process of institutionalization accelerated after the destruction in 70 C.E. As Ronald Green writes, "With the development of village or urban civilization in the Diaspora . . . the Biblically and Talmudically mandated requirements of aid to the poor, comprised under the two headings of *gemiluth chasadim* [voluntary acts of charity] and *ts'dakah* [enforceable obligations of justice] became the responsibility of special communal institutions."[18] This does not mean that the rabbinic discussions did not analyze the rural or agricultural biblical provisions. For example, we raised the question earlier of the size of a "corner" (*peah*). It is not prescribed in Scripture, but the rabbis rule that it should not be less than one-sixtieth of the field but should not be *limited* to that specification. It should be in accord with needs (the number of poor people to be served) and with the yield of the harvest.[19]

Here is an intimation of the balance that marks the detailed regulations in the Talmud. The discussion is pursued and the *halacha* developed in response to a two-fold aim: to see to it that the poor receive sufficient help, and to guard against victimization of the community.

The major devices utilized from the rabbinic period up to the dawn of modern times were the *Tamchui*, or "plate," for the distribution of food, and the *Kuppa*, or "chest," for the distribution of money.

In all the regulations, as in the provision of a Chamber of the Silent, the tradition shows a deep regard for the sensibilities of the deprived. The concern is to avoid humiliating the needy by ostentatious giving or publicly placing a gift in the hand of one of the deprived. Loving kindness is esteemed even above justice, although we are constantly reminded that the aid given to the needy is theirs by right, and is not to be given as a demonstration of benevolence.[20] Yet the high value placed on benevolence can be seen in the often-repeated statement that almsgiving and deeds of loving kindness are equivalent to all the other *mitzvot* together.[21]

Maimonides (1135–1204 C.E.), regarded in the normative tradition as the greatest of the philosophers and codifiers, brings into focus the rabbinic attitude to those who are without worldly resources. In his great work summarizing the whole range of Jewish obligations *(Mishneh Torah*—the Code of Jewish Law), he succeeded in presenting both the rationality and the deeply compassionate nature of the halachic responses to the social inequities of his time. His treatise *Matnot Aniyim*, "gifts or giving" to the poor, draws upon the biblical and talmudic tradition and notes as a transgression "turning one's eyes away" from a poor man who is begging.[22] We are commanded to give a poor man what he lacks in the measure to which he had been accustomed (even to providing him a horse and a manservant to run before him, as Hillel was said to have done).[23] One feeds a poor man who says he is hungry without the delay of examining him to see if he is an impostor. One must feed and clothe the non-Jewish poor as well as the Israelite poor *mip'ney dar-chey shalom*—on behalf of human welfare; one who refuses to give can be compelled to do so by the rabbinical court. Maimonides adds, on the basis of his own observations, the following testimony to the fact that almsgiving was communally institutionalized everywhere among Jews: "We have never seen nor heard of an Israelite community that does not have an alms-fund (*Kuppah*)."[24]

As frequently quoted as they are universally esteemed are Maimonides' eight degrees in the practice of almsgiving.[25] The lowest form is to give reluctantly—with a frowning countenance. The next-higher rung is to give cordially but insufficiently. Above this is giving sufficiently but only when requested. Next higher is to give sufficiently before any request is made. The fourth highest on the scale is to give in such a manner that the giver does not know the recipient. Even more meritorious is to give in a way that prevents the recipient from knowing who the giver is. The second- highest form is the provision of a communal arrangement through which the giver and recipient are not known to one another as in the "Chamber of the Silent." But the highest form of *ts'dakah* is to place the poor person through "a loan, a partnership or a job" in a position that will make it possible for him to become financially independent "and not be forced to the dreadful alternative of holding out his hand for charity."

The essence of these commands is their motivation: respect for human beings. All of them are created in the image of God. One does not humiliate or browbeat another person whether or not one stands in a position of authority or advantage.

This same controlling value affects employer-employee relations as we have seen in other aggadic examples. "You shall not oppress your brother" becomes the basis for a talmudic attempt to define "oppression" (*oshek*). "Anyone who withholds the wages of a hired laborer, transgresses five commandments, as follows: "You shall not oppress your neighbor or rob him; You shall not oppress a poor hired servant; You shall not keep the wages of a hired worker all night; You shall give him his pay on the day [on which he has earned it]; the sun shall not go down upon it." But you shall not oppress or rob? What is the difference between them? One who puts off paying by saying "Go and come back later" or "Go and come again" is guilty of *oshek* (oppression). One who refuses to pay is guilty of *gazel* (robbery). Even the act of causing a person worry and the humiliation of coming back again and again for what is due him is *oshek*.[26]

The distinction between a hired servant and a slave is not always clear, because as we have already indicated, the same word is used for both. But the responsibility to show respect for the "image" even with a slave is clear throughout the rabbinic tradition.[27]

A different kind of concern is displayed with regard to protecting the environment against destruction or pollution, although it reflects the same humane values as those seen in the protection of persons. It is humanity in its divinely ordained role as guardian of the earth[28] that is ultimately affected by its failure to carry that role properly. Some ecological injunctions, indeed, specifically guard persons. Among them are the rules that deal, in simplistic form to be sure, with air pollution. Threshing floors, tanneries, cemeteries, and dumps for the disposal of carcasses must be placed at a distance (50 cubits?) from the borders of towns or cities and must be on the east side so that, in the land of Israel at least, the prevailing winds will carry away the debris or the offensive odors.[29] There is even a provision in the Torah for the disposal of human waste by burial, motivated perhaps by concern for ritual purity but certainly attended by at least a rudimentary consideration for health.[30]

The major talmudic category with respect to ecology is called *bal tashḥit*—"you shall not destroy"—and it is scripturally based on the prohibition in Deuteronomy (20:19–20) against cutting down fruit trees in the course of laying siege to a city. The rabbis develop the principle embodied in this command into a code of conduct governing the role of human beings as guardians of our world.[31] In the Torah, the command is tied to military requirements—but the halachic interpretations by the rabbis extend the provision to guard against wanton destruction in peacetime as well. Destruction is not only that which is done with an axe. Failing to provide adequate irrigation or any other wasteful or destructive act is also regarded as transgressing *bal tashḥit*.[32] Admittedly, the chief social value of protecting the earth against destructive acts of human beings is not always clear in the halachic discussions of the subject. It is undeniably present in the general Jewish outlook and underlies contemporary Jewish aversion to the degradation of forests and wildlife and Jewish support of the efforts of environmentalists to avert the larger dangers of ozone depletion and nuclear destruction.

Although a distinction must be made between the social services offered in the pre-emancipation ghetto communities and the far more sophisticated social services of today, it must be recognized that the contemporary network of Jewish agencies had its roots in the institutions created in their isolation by premodern Jews. Every Jewish settlement had some form of home for the elderly (*moshav z'kenim*) and a transient hostel for wayfarers (*hekdesh*). The duty of affording hospitality to transients fell on individual householders. It was a *mitzvah* to bring a guest home from the synagogue to partake of the family's Sabbath dinner (*hachnasat orchim*), and synagogues themselves provided refuge for the homeless—a practice recently revived in response to the plague of contemporary homelessness. The support of Talmud students who attended the schools of higher Jewish learning away from home was effected by the custom known as "eating days."[33]

These were values and devices that in their simplicity could be maintained by Jewish communities during the long night of exile. The larger concerns were not abandoned: they were made inoperable by the social and political situation. The crumbling of absolutist regimes saw a significant transformation in the Jewish application of major social values.

Through the entire period of Jewish statelessness, from the year 70 C.E. at least until the so-called emancipation at the end of the eighteenth and beginning of the nineteenth century, those social values that related to government or matters of political administration, and to international affairs, war and peace, were theoretical matters—for discussion only. The same was true in the case of rabbinic debate on capital punishment. Occasional limited autonomy in internal affairs permitted the rabbinical courts (*batei din*) to function and to exercise influence on interpersonal relationships. Jews who had disagreements about financial matters, or about damages, or about cases concerning property, slander, or torts, brought their litigation to the *bet din* or to the individual rabbi rather than to the civil courts—a practice that survives to this day among the more pious.[34] There, matters were and are settled according to the dictates of the *halachah*. But when it came to affairs of state, the rivalries and wars of kings and princes and what we today are likely to call "social problems," Jews (except in some notable and atypical instances) had no access to them. At best, they could pray, as they did daily, for a world of equality, freedom, peace, and justice that was free of hunger, deprivation, and violence. But they could do little about it other than to seek to lead their own lives and govern the affairs of their own Jewish communities in accord with the overarching value of *kiddush hashem*, and in accordance with the *mitzvot*. When the ghetto bars were lifted and European Jews became, in increasing measure, participants in democratic society, the repressed drives and instincts for social betterment found them enlisting in disproportionate numbers in movements for change and for justice. The twentieth century also saw the rise of religiously motivated Jewish committees and organizations formed to struggle for specific social ends.

The Central Conference of American Rabbis formed its first committee on a social justice theme in 1910, a seed that grew into the dynamic Religious Action Center of the Commission on Social Action of Reform Judaism.[35] David Einhorn and Bernard Felsenthal both jeopardized their pulpits and their physical safety in action against slavery. A generation later, Emil G. Hirsh, whom we have quoted earlier,[36] and Stephen S. Wise joined in supporting the 1919 strike against U.S. Steel and in supporting the eight-hour working day. Hirsch was the author of the final paragraph in a platform for Reform Judaism adopted in Pittsburgh in 1885, which declared:

> *In full accord with the spirit of Mosaic legislation which strives to regulate the relation between rich and poor, we deem it our duty to participate in the great task of modern times, to solve on the basis of justice and righteousness, the problems presented by the contrasts and evils of the present organization of society.*[37]

This statement of religious motivation for social concern was translated from rhetoric into practice. Jewish women's organizations such as the National Federation of Temple Sisterhoods and the National Council of Jewish

Women not only were early battlers for international peace and human rights, but they also have spurred their large memberships to direct activity in social causes. The Religious Action Center is today effectively engaged in legislative witnessing, education, and protest on the entire front of social concern, and several new projects have spun off from its work.

Most recently, an innovative and independent organization was created—an organization that is building on an idea conceived by Leonard Fein, a dedicated layman, writer, and academician, and enlisting representatives from all segments of American Jewry. It is called *Mazon*, the Hebrew word for "sustenance," and its purpose is to feed the hungry. It urges Jews to add 3 percent to the cost of their happy occasions and their solemn gatherings and to contribute that small increment to *Mazon*; *Mazon* then allocates the funds to communal agencies, of all faiths and ethnic groups, that have shown themselves to be "effective in providing for those who are hungry." With extremely low administrative costs, *Mazon*'s distribution has risen in a few short years to a six-digit figure.

Jewish organizations, and individuals motivated by them, played an active role in the civil rights struggle, their concern for the rights of blacks generated by the inherited social value of human equality. And support for Cesar Chavez's effort to organize migrant agricultural workers was strengthened, interestingly enough, by a direct appeal to the *halachah*. California grapes were declared to be non-Kosher on the principle of *oshek*—oppression—which we have just discussed, bringing significant assistance to the grape boycott through a modern *mitzvah*.

It may well be that the knowledge that one has contributed something to society and has done something *l'takayn et ha-olam*, to improve the world, is the source of the greatest satisfaction. And if, as some have said, value is in the satisfaction of a want, then action on behalf of humanity is quite possibly the highest value.

6
A More Perfect World?

To my knowledge, the question "Can we build a more perfect world?" has never been raised in the history of normative Jewish thought. For Jews to have answered it in the negative would have had a disastrous effect on the whole enterprise. The struggle to make the world a reflection of God's dominion was the task to which they had been called and the goal to which they brought the full power of *emunah*—faithful persistence against all odds in struggling to make God's presence felt. This was *kiddush ha-hayyim*,[1] which must ultimately lead to the fulfillment of God's word, which "never returns void."[2]

Certainly it was the height of presumption for this powerless, relatively minuscule people to see themselves as called to so gigantic a task. They themselves recognized that fact. In the book of Deuteronomy, a sensitive writer ascribed to God a love that was not based on numbers or any special merit but on a historical relationship and a promise that God had made. And in rabbinic fancy, the people of Israel were God's last resort.[3] The nations of the world were all given the opportunity to accept the Torah, and they refused it. They had all asked in turn, "What is written in it?" The children of Esau said "no" when they learned that it contained the command "Thou shalt not murder," because, they said, they lived by the sword. Ammon and Moab refused because of the prohibition of adultery. Ishmael was negative because the Torah contained the words "Thou shalt not steal." And so when God came finally to Israel—the least numerous and least powerful of the nations, and God's last choice—they leaped to accept God's Word, saying, "We will do and we will listen," undertaking to follow it before they knew what was written in it. The usual order is first to listen and then to act. Elsewhere, a "Sadducee" reproaches the Jewish people as an *am p'ziza*—"an impetuous people"—for having put their mouths ahead of their ears (saying "We will do" before "We will listen").[4]

If, as the tradition itself hints, it was presumptuous of the people of Israel to undertake this task, then it must be said that it was a blessed kind of *chutzpah* (which, says Rabbi Naḥman, works even when it is directed against heaven!).[5] The remarkable character of its presumptuousness is underscored by the fact that the full meaning of its mission did not dawn on Israel until it was at the lowest point of its national history—the period of the Babylonian Exile and the return to a seemingly impossible task of rebuilding out of ruins. The great unknown prophet whom we call "Second Isaiah" saw this. It was, paradoxically, the weakness of Israel that made it fit to be the "Servant of God." Scarred, deformed, and degraded, so frail that they could not even quench a dimly burning wick or break a reed that was already bruised, the people of Israel were nonetheless able to persevere in their mission. They would not "cry aloud . . . in the streets" but simply by the power of their commitment and the force of their example they would "make the right to go forth," appointed to be a "covenant-people—a light to the nations" . . . "opening the blind eyes and rescuing prisoners from the prison-house."[6]

The miraculously unexpected occurred and the people that had been beaten and humiliated returned, restored their polity, and rebuilt the Temple. That same miracle was repeated in a fashion unparalleled in human history when that people returned again after a second destruction five hundred years later and a second exile of eighteen hundred years' duration and created a state again. Through the centuries in daily prayer and ritual they clung to the conviction that redemption would come. Against all odds and attended by obstacles that seemed insurmountable, they brought the impossible to pass. There is something paradigmatic in history when we ask ourselves whether the idea that we can create a world of peace and justice is a will-o'-the-wisp, a pursuit of the unattainable, or should still command our commitment and elicit our best efforts. When the practical founder of the modern movement of return called Zionism, Theodore Herzl, embarked on his task, he declared, "If you will it, it is not a *märchen* [fairy tale]." This was the motto inscribed on the title page of his utopian novel, *Altneuland*. He even predicted the half-century span that would elapse before it was recognized that at Basle he had "founded the Jewish State."[7]

Have the last three millennia brought progress? Can we speak of a widening pool of expectations or of judgments based on the social values of our shared tradition?

We posited in our first chapter the view that values are neither words nor ideas but rather the complex of factors that determines choices and decision making. If this can be said of an individual's values, can the same be said of social values? The values of an individual human being can be observed in what that person does. The values of a group, it can be said with equal certainty, are validated as they are expressed in the group's behavior. Henry Margenau's principle for the validation of a cultural group's values was that the group's *behavior* would have to be observed over a period of many centuries.[8] How does a society or a cultural group *act* on its values?

Another remarkable historical fact about Jewish *emunah*, which we have defined as persistent faithfulness, was the high degree of positive correlation between Jewish values and Jewish conduct. We have already cited the testimony of records kept by Jewish communities.[9] Supporting evidence could be marshaled that would show how in the midst of communities and societal groupings in which Jewish social values were rejected, Jews held to those very values in their conduct. A compelling example is offered by Professor S. D. Goitein.[10] It is an example drawn from a medieval Muslim setting, but we could as easily cite the massacres, the blood libels, the false accusations, and the forced conversions of Jews in "Christian" Europe through which, and despite which, the Jews retained their distinctive value stance—for "sufferance is the badge of all our tribe."

Goitein discusses the *issur* or ban on polygamy issued by Rabbenu Gershom of Mayence (Mainz) about the year 1000 C.E. and cites evidence that monogamy had been the established practice among Jews in both Christian and Islamic areas before the ban was promulgated; further, it was a regular part of Jewish marriage contracts found in the Cairo *qenizah* (ca. 950–1250 C.E.). He writes:

> *Another clause that was most often connected with it (the monogamy clause) was one prohibiting the husband from keeping a maidservant whom his wife disliked. To be sure, sexual relations with a slave girl were strictly forbidden by Jewish (as by Christian) law. The new provision aimed at further protection of the wife and the preservation of domestic peace* (shalom bayit). *In view of the extensive concubinage practiced by the Muslim majority, this was a particularly difficult task; but as proved by the rich documentation of the* genizah *it must have been carried out satisfactorily to a remarkable degree.*

Goitein also informs us that, because of the size of the Jewish communities at that time in Islamic countries, Jewish civil law, unlike that of Christian Europe, "was also largely the domain of the Jewish courts and therefore an area for the development of human rights."[11] This ability to withstand the corrupting influence of the environment is another example of the power of *mitzvah* in the life of the organic Jewish community.

Most of the conduct to which we refer as persistently faithful was carried out in response not to halachic, scripturally founded ordinances but rather to injunctions based upon a concern for general human welfare: *mip'nay tikkun ha-olam*.

Tikkun ha-olam, literally the mending or improvement of the world, like all cluster words and phrases has had a long and complex technical development. Contemporary usage adopts the meaning the phrase has received in the classical prayer book in all trends of Judaism—such as in the *Alenu:* "We are obliged to praise the Lord of All . . ." The first part of this was probably composed about the year 200 C.E., and since the fourteenth century it has been universally recited as the concluding prayer in every public worship service. The relevant words of this solemn expression of hope in a this-worldly eschatology date back at least to the ninth century and probably earlier.[12] They are (in a literal translation): "We therefore hope in Thee, O Lord our God that we may speedily see the glory of Thy might, when Thou wilt remove abominations from the earth and pagan idols will be completely destroyed so that the world will be perfected into the Kingdom of God and all human beings will call upon Thy name." The Hebrew phrase is *l'takeyn olam b'malchut shaddai*—to repair or improve the world until the dominion of the Almighty is established. The conclusion of the *Alenu* confidently proclaims that "on that day the Lord will be one and his name will be one." That this prayer was frequently the subject of misunderstanding and the object of action by Christian censors is an irony of liturgical history.[13] But modern Jewish thought, with much warrant from the commentaries on this prayer, exalts the concept of *tikkun ha-olam* as the major goal of Jewish existence—the world mission of the Jew.

The phrase itself appears nowhere in Scripture. The verb *l'takayn* is used in Ecclesiastes,[14] where the meaning is "to set [something] straight" or "to arrange in order." In rabbinic use, it means to establish or to ordain as in the great paradox mentioned in Tractate *B'rachot*[15] that "on the very day on which permission was given to bury those who died at Bethar" (which was the last stand of Bar Kochba's second-century revolt against the Romans and thus the moment of extinction of Jewish national sovereignty for 1800 years) they ordained (*tik-nu*) in Yavneh that the blessing "God who is good and doeth good" should be recited in the grace after meals.

In rabbinic literature the words occur most frequently in the phrase *mip'nay tikkun ha-olam*,[16] which sometimes is invoked with reference to acts of individual probity, sometimes to societal devices deemed necessary (e.g., Hillel's *prosbul*),[17] and sometimes to actions performed because of general welfare considerations.[18]

The contention of some that the phrase means "for the proper order of the Jewish community" flies in the face of the fact that the word *olam* is always invested with a universal or general meaning. (This is the case even in Yiddish, where the word *oylem* means the undifferentiated mass—*die oylem iz a goylem*, which might be translated "the masses are like a medieval robot"—and where a hyperbole for "everything" is *oylem u'm'lo-o*.) What the phrase *tikkun ha-olam* has come to mean in modern Jewish colloquial use is indisputable. It contains the meaning given it, as we have said, in the *Alenu* prayer. Eugene Lipmann, despite his conclusions in his penetrative essay on the subject, concedes that "the phrase is used in our time as a major *mitzvah* for contemporary Jews and for the Jewish community: to move the entire world toward our universalistic goals."[19] But on the basis of the evidence presented by its use in the liturgy, that meaning has been present for at least one thousand years. As for the Jewish commitment to the building of the divine dominion on earth and the consequent "better world," that concept, as we have demonstrated, goes back at the very least to the era of the prophets of Israel.

One of the universalistic goals to which the obligation

of *tikkun* is dedicated—and possibly the most important of those goals—is the achievement of harmonious relations among human beings. What needs correction or mending by its elimination is the blight of racism. If "racism" means "the assignment of different degrees of value—dignity, capacity, entitlement—to kinship groups" and "asserts that these qualitative distinctions justify discrimination in assignment of rights," then it is true that there is no racism in the Bible or in postbiblical Jewish thought and action up to modern times.[20] How could there be, when the Jewish people have been multiracial from earliest times? The Hebrews were, according to most recent scholarly conjecture, an amalgamation of unlanded, stateless individuals drawn from several different kinship groups. Amos, in his eloquent espousal of God's universality, charges the people of Israel that they are no different from the Ethiopians in the sight of God. We don't know whether Amos selected the Ethiopians along with the Aramaeans and Philistines as an example of how *far* the love and care of God extend or whether he was conscious of a color-difference. The admixture of converts of every ethnic background added to the multiplicity of types among Jews. The black Jews of Cochin, the brown Bene Israel of Bombay, the Yemenites, and the Ethiopian Jews of today have all been received in the State of Israel as Jews under the law of return.[21] Jewish tradition has always taken for granted the surpassing beauty of the Shulamite maiden in the "Song of Songs." "I am black *and* I am beautiful," she sings.[22] The large number of Jews who participated in the American struggle for civil rights for blacks testifies to the abiding power of social values born in tradition and developed in historic experience. Some Jews who went to Mississippi in 1964 to aid the voter registration campaign were beaten, and at least two were killed.[23] The American Jewish Congress and the Religious Action Center for Reform Judaism played significant roles in aiding the struggle against discrimination, segregation and oppression.

Quoting from an unpublished manuscript, S. D.

Goitein cites a statement by Solomon ben Judah, the eleventh-century head of the Jerusalem yeshivah, who appealed for human rights with a reference to Malachi 2:10—"Do we not all have one father . . . ?" and adds, "The Father alluded to here is not Abraham, the Father of the Faith, but Adam, the Father of mankind."[24]

Another goal for which *tikkun* is required is the building of a world in which poverty with its attendant hunger and homelessness will be no more. This is one goal that should be within our reach, because our earth is capable of providing food and shelter even for its swollen population, capable of providing a social structure in which all people will sit under their own "vines and fig trees with none to make them afraid." It is, however, a goal the achievement of which is blocked by economic and systemic complexities that have baffled the best intentions of the best minds and the best planners. From the Deuteronomist to Karl Marx, from the Kropotkins to the Henry Georges, from the supporters of free enterprise to the proponents of the welfare state—no one has yet been successful. Even the balanced efforts toward full employment and equitable distribution have been frustrated in a rising tide of hunger and homelessness in our own democratic and supposedly benevolent society.[25] Even in the simple agricultural society of biblical Israel, the conviction arose, as if it were a mandatory condition, that "the poor will always be with us."[26] Shelters, breadlines, and soup kitchens are palliatives and bandaids. Utopia continues to elude us. The slack in our society —rather a yawning crevice—still has to be met with philanthropic enterprise, which is always inadequate to the total task; and the *k'vod ha-bri'yot*, the dignity of God's creatures that we seek to ensure, founders for lack of an effective solution—although not for lack of will.

The goal of equal rights for women is one not too difficult to bring to full realization. It requires that opening of the eyes that women's movements have felicitously called "consciousness raising." The role of language in presenting the attitudes that make it a "man's world" is not inconsiderable. We may hold that "man" and "mankind" are generic terms in which both sexes are included, and they frequently are—certainly in our legal tradition and in our basic democratic documents as well as in the first chapter of the book of Genesis; but it must be confessed that in business, the arts, and the sciences, sexist language has been instrumental in excluding women from male preserves that should be open to all. Linguistically we have not yet gotten over the awkwardness of terms such as "chairperson" (or worse, "chair"), the male personifications of the divine in liturgy, or the discomfort of his-or-her pronouns in academic papers and books.

The term "women's liberation," however, has never been apt with respect to Jewish thought. Sara, Rebecca, Rachel, and Leah were never mere chattels—they were full-blown personalities with managerial rights and capacities. The daughters of Zelophehad won their case with Moses and secured their rights of inheritance.[27] True, the male had greater sexual freedom than the female, but it was for the most part a technical freedom. In neither biblical culture nor in dispersion did a society that showed reciprocal sexual respect permit him to exercise it. And when as in the biblical tale of Judah he did so he was the dupe of the supremely clever and determined Tamar.[28] Where is there a greater paean to women's independence and practical leadership than in the thirty-first chapter of the book of Proverbs? She is a vigorous woman who presides over her household with strength and dignity (an *eshet chayil*, v. 10). She is optimistic, perhaps even possessing a sense of humor (v. 25); she works with wool and flax (v. 13) and oversees the provision of food to her household—which includes domestic servants—getting up while it is still dark to do so (v. 15). She buys real estate and manages a vineyard (v. 16); she stays up late working at her business affairs and her textile making (vv. 18, 19); she handles the household's *ts'daka* (v. 20); and she is a wise and effective teacher (v. 26).

And what does her husband do? He sits in the broad place of the city gate with his cronies and boasts about his wonderful wife (vv. 23, 29, 30)!

We are not told in this hyperbolic song how she survives such a schedule, even though her children (she is also a mother!) declare her happy (v. 28). Nevertheless, it does present the picture of an idealized matriarchal society—a picture emulated by Jewish women of the ghetto and *shtetl* communities who labored in the market place and were the family providers so that their husbands might study Torah. But certainly this is not the kind of "liberation" a modern woman wants—"liberation" means the *sharing* of responsibility with a partner, not carrying the whole load while the man luxuriates in his leisure.

The Bible, says Herbert Brichto, is not a textbook of male chauvinism. Israelite society resembled Mesopotamian society, where, he contends, there were exceptionally high standards of "dignity and entitlements" for women.[29] S. D. Goitein points out that Jewish women's rights in Islamic lands and generally elsewhere were stringently protected in the *ketubah* (the marriage contract), in which the condition was inserted that the husband stood surety with all his possessions, real and mobile, and "even the coat from his shoulder."[30] It should be noted that a Jewish wife could bring her husband before the rabbinic court for punishment, for redress, or even for divorce.

This is not to say that it was an ideal situation for Jewish women. The entire society in which they lived was male-oriented. But the Jewish values of respect and compassion and the unwillingness to see the woman as anything less than a full human being were reflected in the technical arrangements made for her protection.

No goal that is set for the task of *tikkun* receives greater attention and greater praise than those given to the value of peace and the injunctions to work for it. "Be ye disciples of Aaron, loving peace and pursing peace, loving human beings and bringing them near to the Torah" is the very first aphorism of Hillel the Elder.[31] Love peace, the rabbis said, where you are and pursue it everywhere else.[32]

Unlike the word "peace," the Hebrew word *shalom* has positive content. "Peace" means the absence of struggle and is essentially a negative term. *Shalom* includes the sense of wholeness and security. The common conversational gambit in modern colloquial Hebrew, *Mah sh'lom-cha?* ("What is your *shalom?*"), means "How are you doing?" or "What is your total condition?"[33]

The yearning for peace in both Scripture and rabbinic literature is a yearning for that messianic state described by Micah as a time not only when the weapons of war will be destroyed but also when everyone will dwell without fear under his or her own "vine and fig tree."

Neither the Bible nor the Talmud can be characterized as pacifist in an absolute sense. The tradition—dealing to be sure with questions that were moot in a time when Jews had no state and no power—makes room for "discretionary" wars, obligatory wars, and wars of defense.[34] But there is no mistaking the abhorrence of violence that runs through rabbinic literature as a direct derivative from the high value attached to life and its sanctity.[35] Indeed, *sh'fichut damim*, bloodshed, as we have already pointed out, is one of three cardinal sins that one should avoid even at the cost of one's life. We could multiply examples of the rabbinic emphasis on this value. "The whole Torah was given for the purpose of promoting peace." As it is said (Prov. 3:17), "Her ways are ways of pleasantness and all its paths are peace."[36]

For one, Scripture includes a form of conscientious objection when it exempts from military service a new bridegroom, a new householder, and one who is "fearful and fainthearted"[37] Fearful and fainthearted? The rabbis seize on the tautology and say that fainthearted does not mean afraid of being killed, but rather afraid of being forced to kill.[38]

In another example, a discussion of whether weapons may be carried on the Sabbath produces a consensus of the sages that they may not be carried—not on the ground that they are an adornment, but on the ground that they are a disgrace.[39] And as a proof text they invoke the word of Isaiah: "they shall beat their swords into ploughshares . . ." (2:4).

King David, who is depicted in the Bible as a bandit chief and whose propensity for violence is not covered up by the writers of Scripture, appears in rabbinic literature as a scholar who rises at midnight to study and as a sweet singer of psalms.

At the *seder*, the Passover meal, the wicked son who separates himself from the community of Israel is depicted in illustrated *haggadot* as a military man with armor and weapons.

The reluctance to take up arms except in self-defense is illustrated by the history of the *Hagana*, created by the Jews in Palestine before the establishment of the State. *Hagana* means "defense." It was a paramilitary force governed by a strict code that prohibited preemptive or first-strike action.[40]

Perhaps the most poignant and distressing value conflict relevant here is that into which the newly reborn State of Israel has been plunged. There the very real longing for peace, after so much blood and tears, conflicts with the very real fear that the security and preservation of the state are threatened. In this fear and in the determination to prevent the destruction of the State, the citizens of Israel are joined by the Jews of the Diaspora. Yet among them, both within the land and outside the land, there are deep divisions of opinion between hard-liners and accommodationists. It is not the facile distinction between "doves" and "hawks" that the media so simplistically promote. The scale of differences includes every shade of opinion, from the Greater Israel adherents whose firm devotion to the retention of Judaea and Samaria has the support of one-half of the Israeli populace, to a line of increasing openness to some measure of accommodation to those peace advocates who risk violating the law in conversing with representatives of the Palestine Liberation Organization. Meanwhile, we have the strange phenomenon of challenges to the nonviolent aspects of our heritage and to the social values of Jewish tradition coming from the *haredim*, the extreme Orthodox who opposed the establishment of the State and would now like to convert it from the democratic society it currently is, into a rigid and intolerant theocracy.

Where, then, is the source of hope that would make *tikkun ha-olam* a viable enterprise? Paradoxically, it lies in the fact that we can always count on change, that nothing is forever. This ancient doctrine of Heraclitus is echoed in sophisticated form in the teachings of Ernst Bloch, the Marxist Jewish-born philosopher from whom the noted Protestant theologian Jürgen Moltmann acknowledgedly took his "Theology of Hope." Bloch theorizes that there is that which can be called the *noch nicht sein*—that which has not yet come into being. History, he maintains, is constantly throwing up events that are totally unexpected—the *novum*, the new thing that changes the situational complex in which we find ourselves.[41]

This idea is not without precedent in Jewish thought. Again and again, the people of Israel have gone from the *Emek Habacha*, the vale of tears, through the *Petah Tikva*, the door of hope. Despair is a major sin. It is the antithesis of the *emunah*, the persistent faithfulness that has characterized the Jewish millennial journey. In the midst of the most bitter deprivations, the Jew has proclaimed *Ashrenu! Mah tov helkenu!*—"Happy are we! How good is our lot!" And the prophet of comfort and encouragement, the great Second Isaiah, whose entire message is one of hope, portrays God as saying, "*Hineni oseh hadasha* " (43:19)—"Behold I am doing a new thing!"[42]

The times in which we live have given dramatic testimony to the role of change in producing a new and hopeful set of factors. In recent years, witness the changes in the former Soviet Union, the victory of Solidarity and the breaching of the iron wall of communism in Poland, the proclamation of a democratic republic in Hungary, the miraculous rescue of almost 14,000 Jews in Ethiopia, and the epoch-making and heroic pilgrimage to Jerusalem by Anwar Sadat. All these changes were totally unexpected and unforeseen.

Nearly fifty years ago, the recognition of the State of Israel and its rebirth took by surprise even those of us who were confidently asserting its inevitability. With tears of joy and with a sense of its miraculous aptness, we sang the psalm written for the first return some 2300 years earlier: "When the Lord turned the captivity of Zion, we were like dreamers. Our mouths were filled with song."[43] The nations stood amazed, the psalmist continues, and conceded the greatness of what had happened, recognizing that those who sow in tears may often reap in joy.

Dreams are not to be disparaged. When the dreamers are fully committed and willing to labor and sacrifice, dreams are often fulfilled. In the words of Saul Tchernichovski, the poet of the Hebrew renaissance,

> *You can laugh at all my dreams, my dear one,*
> *Laugh but I repeat anew*
> *That I still believe in Man*
> *as I still believe in you.*
>
> *Let the times be dark with hatred*
> *I believe in years beyond*
> *Love at last will bind the peoples*
> *In an everlasting bond.*[44]

Can we build a better world? The answer, as in the old fable, is in our hands.

Epilogue

As I review the words of hope with which I concluded my survey, I am reminded of the tenacity of evil. Recall the Persian Gulf War, and the threatened destruction of the State of Israel. What does this do to our thesis? That the Jewish outlook has always clung to the promise of a better time cannot be questioned. Despair is a cardinal sin, as we have already written. The fundamental meaning of *emunah* is "never give up!"[1]

But the conviction that there could be a better future has always been attended by reservations. First, the future had two faces. Second, the end-time fulfillment was not immediately at hand. Third, redemption would come slowly, bit by bit. And fourth, it was dependent on human effort.

Two faces? Amos warned his generation that the "Day of the Lord" for which they were waiting would be a day of darkness and not light, a day of doom brought on by their sins (5:18); and Zephaniah echoed that grim prediction, foretelling a day of wrath and trouble, of clouds and thick darkness (1:15). But Isaiah/Micah envision a future time of peace and security for all mankind (Isaiah 2; Micah 4). This quite understandable ambivalence makes its way into the rabbinic tradition. There is a note of caution: don't be too certain of redemption and certainly don't try to calculate when it will come.[2]

When Rabbi Akiba hailed as the Messiah Bar Kochba,

the warrior who led a remarkable and temporarily successful revolt against Rome in the second century C.E., he was cautioned, "Grass will grow out of your chin, Akiba, before you see the Messiah." The pragmatic view was expressed as well. "If there is a plant in your hand, and you are told 'Behold the Messiah is here,' first go and do your planting, then go to welcome the Messiah."[3]

Even though redemption was certain, it would not burst upon the world all at once. This was the dictum of two of the leading sages of their generation, Rabbi Ḥiyya the Great and Rabbi Shim'on ben Ḥalafta: "This is what the redemption of Israel is like—at first it will come little by little by little—but as it continues it will grow greater."[4]

Indeed, the idea that redemption must be incremental comports with human experience. Progress is, we must believe, discernible, even though there are disappointments and setbacks.

As for the conviction that redemption is dependent on human effort, there is a host of apothegms and reflections that can be cited. "When will the Messiah come?" The answer is, "When we ourselves bring him!" As an instance of what was meant, it was said that when all Israel keeps one Sabbath perfectly, the Messiah will come—or, better, will have come.

A tale about a pious *Ḥasid* is instructive in this connection. He yearned so much for the coming of the Messiah that he wanted to be among the first to greet him. Believing that he would appear on the Mount of Olives, he journeyed to Jerusalem and settled in a little shack close to the Mount. There he listened for the blast on the ram's horn that would proclaim the Messiah's arrival, and he waited. Word of his obsession leaked out and he fell prey to a prankster who one day at dawn went up on the Mount, took a ram's horn and blew a mighty *tekiah g'dolah*, a great and sustained call suitable to the pretended occasion. The *Ḥasid* awoke, rushed to the window, and surveyed the scene. The first thing he saw was a carter beating his donkey. "This is no messianic world," he said. And he went back to bed.

An anecdote in the Talmud underscores the same conviction. A sage meets Elijah the prophet, who in Jewish folklore plays a role in happy celebrations and in solving difficult problems. The sage asks Elijah, "When will the Messiah come?"

"Go and ask him," says Elijah.

"And where will I find him?" asks the sage.

"He is sitting in the city gate among the poor lepers."

"And how will I know him?" says the sage.

Elijah answers, "He is the one who is constantly unwinding and re-doing his bandages (so as to be ready, when called)."

And the rabbi goes and seeks him out. "Are you the Messiah?" he asks.

"You have said it," the beggar replies.

"When will you come?" asks the sage.

"Today," he answers. The rabbi returns home in great excitement to prepare for the coming of the Messiah—but nothing happens. When he next encounters Elijah, he complains, "He lied to me! He said he would come today but he didn't come."

"Ah!" said Elijah, "but you didn't supply the rest of the verse (Psalm 95:7.) It reads, 'Today, if you will hearken to my voice.'"[5]

Rabbinic skepticism goes further. One sage says there will be no Messiah for Israel, that he has already come in the days of Hezekiah. Another offers the opinion that redemption means only release from servitude to foreign nations. All of the calculated dates for redemption have passed. Now redemption is wholly dependent on repentance and good deeds.[6]

There is no assurance. Redemption will tarry, but we are to persist (in *emunah*) in our effort to bring it. In our tangled world scene, change—the unexpected—is our ally.

If we cannot see the hand of providence in the cessation of the cold war and the abatement of hostility between the superpowers, we can at least derive comfort from the timing of events that made possible unprecedented world unity in the Persian Gulf and brought the bruited possibility that the lessons of 1933 have been well learned by the nations. People of goodwill have no alternative but to act with courage and determination and the unabandoned hope that future terrors will be averted without bloodletting and suffering.

In our daily prayer we praise God "Who is the Maker of peace and the Creator of everything"—*oseh shalom u'voray et ha-kol*.[7] The parallelism (typical of Hebrew poetry) indicates that peace is as great as the totality of everything else. The need to bear this in mind is unprecedentedly great.

I am led to reflect on the wisdom of the old insight that the more things change, the more they remain the same. The Gulf War is over, presumably having reached its goal, but Saddam Hussein is still in power, and even as I put these words on paper the United Nations is in ferment following the truculent, intransigent speech of Iraq's representative, the Iraqi Foreign Ministry's defiant position on Iraq's right to determine where its troops shall move, and the deployment of Iraqi armor and a division of Iraq's troops close to the Kuwaiti border. We have witnessed the horror of genocidal slaughter in Rwanda and the continuing brutality and cruelty in Bosnia cloaked in hypocritical euphemisms like "ethnic cleansing."

But our thesis is strengthened. Progress is incremental. The United Nations has provided a peace-keeping presence in both these violence-torn areas and in other trouble spots such as Somalia. Technological advances in communication and transportation have strengthened our conviction that we are truly one world. Change does mean new possibilities, and, sending up its shoots amid the rubble of failure and disappointment, hope is still alive and verdant.

Notes

Introduction

1. On the basis of their survey of Jewish community studies, Steven Cohen and Calvin Goldscheider present, among other findings that Samuel Klausner says are "undisputed," the following conclusions: "about two-thirds of Jewish Americans contribute to Jewish philanthropies (the measure of Jewish gifts to non-Jewish and general philanthropies is also disproportionately high). . . On the whole, American Jewish political ideology remains liberal. Jews continue to vote for candidates of the Democratic party despite their move into the Republican economic class. They favor birth control and the right to abortion and believe in the efficacy of government welfare programs." See Samuel Z. Klausner, "Jewry's Survival in a Time of Depopulation," *Yearbook of the Central Conference of American Rabbis*, vol. XCIX (New York: Central Conference of American Rabbis, 1989), 60. See also Steven M. Cohen, *The Dimensions Jewish Liberalism* (New York: American Jewish Committee, 1989).

2. The bibliography, which follows this section, lists several helpful monographs and studies on various aspects of the subject but no systematic, overall approach to it.

3. Avot V:22. (For a description of Avot and its place in the literature, see chapter 3, pages 38–39.)

4. Erubin 13b.

5. See Ephraim Urbach, *The Sages: Their Concepts and Beliefs* (Jerusalem: Magnes Press, 1975), 549. The statement is attributed to Rabbi Shim'on ben Yohai, who is said to have been speaking

intemperately because of "bitter disillusionary experience." Elsewhere, Rabbi Shim'on exalts love of the stranger, citing a connection between Judges 5:31 and Deuteronomy 10:18f. See Mechilta, chap. XVIII, 1.14 (Lauterbach, Mechilta, III, p. 138 [Jewish Publication Society]; Weiss, Mechilta, 101a). (Reference in Urbach is incorrect.)

6. This is attributed to Rabbi Ḥelbo, a fourth-century *amora* (a teacher cited in the Gemara, the second, post–200 C.E., and larger part of the Talmud) who was probably indulging in a play on words: the word for a scab or an itching sore is *sapachat*, and the same root is found in Isaiah 19:1 for his declaration that "strangers" (the same word comes to mean "converts") will cleave (*nis-p-chu*) to the House of Jacob. See Urbach, *The Sages*, 550; Kiddushin 70b; and Yebamot 109b. The Gemara passages cited seem to take Rabbi Ḥelbo's words seriously. The view of Abraham Ha-ger is reflected in the commentary Tosafot to the passage in Kiddushin 70b (bottom) (contrary to the Rashi ad loc.) in which Israel's dispersion is seen as an instrument for the attraction of converts and that quotes Abraham Ha-ger directly in confirmation of the positive value to Israel that converts bring.

7. See chapter 1, pp. 9–11, 14–15.

8. *Lehren des Judenthums* III, p. 7 (Lelyveld's translation).

9. Leviticus 30:35f. Note that the text extends the same right to the "stranger and the sojourner." See the difficult hypothetical situation posed by a debate on the verse in Baba Metsia 62a.

10. Simon Bernfeld, ed., *Lehren des Judenthums* III, 7.

Chapter 1

1. Taanit 21a. Also Baba Batra 10a, where Rabbi Joshua ben Korḥa is quoted, saying, "Whoever turns his eyes away from [one who appeals for] charity is considered as if he were serving idols."

2. Luke 10:30–37.

3. Leviticus 19:16, 18, 33f.

4. B'midbar Rabba to Numbers 25:17–18.

5. Yoma 82b (bottom).

6. Vayikra Rabba XXVII.5 (Soncino, 347–49).

7. John Dewey, "Field of Value," in *Value: A Cooperative Inquiry*, ed. Ray Lepley (New York: Columbia University Press, 1949), 64f.
8. Ibid.
9. R. M. Hare, *The Language of Morals* (London: Oxford University Press, 1961), 1. "If we want to learn a person's moral principles, we could be most sure of a true answer . . . by studying what he *did*." The tradition affirms that scholars should be judged not by their learning but by their actions. Yoma 86a. See Urbach, *The Sages*, 629.
10. Dewey, in *Value: A Cooperative Inquiry*, 70.
11. *Value: A Cooperative Inquiry*, 312ff.
12. Goethe, *Faust*, pt. I, lines 1699–1700.
13. A. Campbell Garnett, "Critique of John Dewey's 'Field of Values,'" in *Value: A Cooperative Inquiry*, 314.
14. See below, p. 13.
15. Leviticus 11:47 and frequently.
16. Robert S. Hartmann, "The Science of Values," in *New Knowledge in Human Values*, ed. Abraham H. Maslow (New York: Harper, 1959), 14.
17. Ralph Barton Perry, *Realms of Value* (Cambridge, Mass.: Harvard University Press, 1954), 95, 132f. Perry is himself aware of the potential *conflicting* interests.
18. Hartmann, "The Science of Values," 20.
19. Ibid., 60. Cf. Santayana: "It is not wisdom to be only wise and on the inner vision close the eyes"; and Miguel de Unamuno: "Para pensar cual tú, solo es preciso no tener nada más que inteligencia."
20. Paul Tillich, "Is a Science of Human Values Possible?" in *New Knowledge*, 191–93.
21. Ibid., 192.
22. Ibid., 196.
23. See my *Atheism Is Dead* (Cleveland: World Publishing, 1968), 194ff.
24. Henry Margenau, "The Scientific Role of Value Theory," in *New Knowledge*, 42, 44ff.
25. Deuteronomy 20:11–14.
26. Margenau, "Scientific Role," 44.
27. Ibid., 49.
28. A maxim from Aristotle: "Virtue . . . is a disposition

governing our choices." See *Nicomachean Ethics* 1106 (Cambridge, Mass.: Harvard University Press, 1975). Cf. "disposition" with "stance," below.

29. See my "Values and Value Stances," *Congress Bi-Weekly*, April 3, 1967.

30. Nina Bull, *The Attitude Theory of Emotion*, Nervous and Mental Disease Monographs, no. 81 (New York, 1951).

31. See Max Kadushin, *The Rabbinic Mind* (New York: Jewish Theological Seminary, 1952), 2ff, 28, 113, 131. See also Philip Wheelwright, *The Burning Fountain* (Bloomington: Indiana University Press, 1959), 62ff, 25–29.

32. Suzanne Langer, *Philosophy in a New Key* (Cambridge, Mass.: Harvard University Press, 1942), 103ff.

Chapter 2

1. *JTA Community News Reporter*, 30 December 1988 (Jewish Telegraphic Agency, New York).

2. See James A. Matiscoff, *Blessing, Curses, Hopes, and Fears: Psycho-Ostensive Expressions in Yiddish* (Philadelphia: Institute for the Study of Human Issues, 1979), 69ff.

3. Avot I:11.

4. Cynthia Ozick, "America Toward Yavneh," *Congress Bi-Weekly*, 26 Feb. 1971 (e.g., "Why don't you come over *erev shabbos* and join us for *kiddush* . . . you'll be enabling me to do a *mitzvah*").

5. Ḥayyim Greenberg anthology *The Inner Eye*, ed. Marie Syrkin (Detroit: Wayne State University Press, 1968), 178. I have called these words untranslatable, and English equivalents are but approximations of their meaning. *Mitzvah*, for example, is literally "command," but, as will become apparent in what follows, it means so much more that so rendering it distorts its meaning. An *averah* is a "transgression," but again, this fails to convey its tone and its associations; and so with the other examples cited by Greenberg.

6. See my *Atheism Is Dead*, 164ff.

7. *A Dictionary of the Targumim, the Talmud* . . . etc." (New York: Marcus Jastrow, 1950), 1267.

8. Avot IV:2.

9. Although Orthodox Judaism affirms the binding character of all 613 commandments, it is recognized that some are obsolete or in suspension (the commands relating to the Temple in Jerusalem and the sacrificial system, for example) and others are not relevant in our era or to our situation, such as the establishment of cities of refuge for those who have committed involuntary manslaughter (Numbers 35:10ff). Only seven *mitzvot* are incumbent on non-Jews (as well as on Jews)—the so-called Noachide Code derived hermeneutically from Genesis 9, which represents God's demand on all humanity: the prohibition of bloodshed, the establishment of courts of justice, the prohibition of incest and adultery, the prohibition of theft, pagan worship, blasphemy, shedding blood, and the "limb torn from a *living animal*" (eating flesh with the blood in it). See "Noachide Code" in the *Encyclopedia Judaica*.

10. Naḥman of Brazlav. Cited by Abraham Heschel, *God in Search of Man* (Philadelphia: Jewish Publication Society, 1956), 361.

11. See my *Atheism Is Dead*, 130ff.

12. Rudolph Otto, *The Idea of the Holy* (London: Oxford University Press, 1923).

13. E.g., Genesis 3:3.

14. Leviticus 10:1–3.

15. 2 Samuel 6.

16. Gilbert Murray, *Five Stages of Greek Religion* (London: Greenwood Press, 1946), 68.

17. Isaiah 6.

18. Fr. Robert Murray of Heythrop College, University of London, has called my attention to the way the word *k'doshim* is used in Psalm 89:6 as constituting a heavenly council for Yahveh and has referred me to Margaret Barker, *The Older Testament* (London: SPCK, 1987), 111. However, this does not nullify my contention that Isaiah was probably the first to identify the *Kadosh* as the "*Kadosh* of Israel: The Lord of Hosts." The history of the word *kadosh*, antecedent to the revolutionary insight of Isaiah, includes not only what I have described but also the description of male and female temple prostitutes. That it should also be applied to councilors of the Heavenly King need not surprise us. The layers of meaning with which the term is invested are part of its development—and the earlier layers frequently survive in the

term's usage alongside the developed meaning. See my *Atheism Is Dead*, chap. 9, "The Sense of Presence." As for the "celestial retinue," which is the *Bet Din* on High—the heavenly court—its members are never referred to as *k'doshim* in rabbinic literature. See Urbach, *The Sages*, 77ff, 178ff.

19. Isaiah 5:16.
20. Leviticus 19 is generally held to be pre-exilic, possibly seventh century. It is not unlikely, then, that it reflects the teachings of the eighth-century Isaiah of Jerusalem. Compare Korach's defiance of Moses (Num. 16:1ff, esp v. 7): *ki kol ha-edah kulam k'doshim*—The [members of the] entire congregation—all of them are *k'doshim*. (In other words, every human being is the bearer of the divine image.) As for the use of the Hebrew imperfect to express a present and continuing state, see S. P. Driver, *The Use of the Tenses in Hebrew* (London: Oxford University Press, 1892), 37.
21. B'reshit Rabba 24:7 with reference to Genesis 5:2.
22. Yebamot 79a despite its violent context (2 Samuel 21). Urbach comments (*The Sages*, 516ff) that "The sages were perplexed." See below pp. 48ff.
23. Taking advantage of another's ignorance is "putting a stumbling block before the blind." See chap. 4, pp. 52–53.
24. See Makkot 24a and cf. *Die Lehren des Judenthums* III, 27f.
25. Matthew 22:35ff.
26. Talmudic tradition was largely controlled by the school of Hillel, which portrayed Shammai as rigid and irascible. That *bet Shammai* was not always harsh and lacking in humane values is shown below, pp. 49–50. See Jacob Neusner, *First-Century Judaism in Crisis* (New York: K'tav, 1982), 54. Of the 316 recorded controversies between *bet Hillel* and *bet Shammai*, *bet Shammai* is recorded on the lenient side in fifty-five of them. See M. Berachot VIII.
27. The word *shem*, meaning "name," is the usual reverent substitution for direct reference to the deity.
28. See my *Atheism Is Dead*, 137ff and 178ff. The fate of those who died *al kiddush hashem* during the Hadrianic persecution is preserved in legend and liturgy—especially the Roman execution of Akiba and Ḥananiah ben Teradyon. See "Ten Martyrs" in the *Encyclopedia Judaica*.
29. D'varim Rabba III:3.

30. See below, p. 48, for the concept of *lifnim mi-shurat ha-din*—"within the line of the law."

31. Isaiah 1:10–17, 58:6–7.

32. ". . . that your manservant and your maidservant [or, "male and female slaves"] may rest just like you, for you shall remember that you were a slave in the land of Egypt" (Deut. 5:14–15).

33. *Seder Avodat Yisrael*, ed. S. Baer (New York: Schocken, 1937), 555.

34. See Ronald M. Green, *Religion and Moral Reason* (New York: Oxford University Press, 1988), 149–56; and see *The Passover Haggadah* (note 36 below), 10, 49. Green writes: "It is important to note that this identification with the historic Exodus community is not just an implication of the Seder service, but a mandated requirement" (p. 152). "Personal suffering and respect for others go together because those who have been humiliated or oppressed are most alert to the exile a society must avoid [or *should* be alert as Jews are *required* to be]."

He continues: "These links between Exodus *communitas* and devotion to the moral norms governing life in the community, are perhaps less explicit in the Seder liturgy than they are in the biblical sources on which it draws. But these norms form the context of the rite. They are assumed in the special attention given humble guests at the Seder table and they endure in the great emphasis on communal solidarity and support of the poor" (p. 154).

35. Nahum Slouschz, *Travels in North Africa* (Philadelphia: Jewish Publication Society, 1927), 133.

36. See any order of service for the Passover Seder (known as the *Haggadah*: "telling"—e.g., E. D. Goldschmidt, *The Passover Haggadah*, ed. Nahum Glatzer, trans. Jacob Sloan (New York: Schocken, 1969), 10f.

37. S. Baer, *Siddur* (New York: Schocken, 1937), 247.

38. The constant repetition of this "slaves in Egypt" motif (as here: Exod. 22:21) reinforces the ethical expectations that, having experienced suffering, one will be concerned and compassionate when confronted with the suffering of others.

39. See my *A Distinctive Value Stance*, 4f. See also Saul Bellow, *Herzog*, Fawcett Crest edition (New York: Viking Press, 1964), 349f.

40. See C. G. Montefiore, "The Use of Adjectives 'Jewish' and 'Christian' in England," "Excursus I," in Montefiore and Loewe, *A Rabbinic Anthology* (New York: Macmillan, 1938), 60ff.
41. Cf. Kohelet Rabbah to VII:16.
42. "Liberalism and Intelligence," Fourth John Dewey Memorial Lecture, Bennington, Vermont, p. 7.
43. See my *Atheism Is Dead*, 3ff.

Chapter 3

1. M. Sanhedrin 4:5.
2. Ibid.
3. As this was being written, we were witnessing a dramatic overturn in the Soviet Union and in the Marxist societies of Eastern Europe. Gorbachev's introduction of *glasnost* and the concept of *perestroika* were a belated recognition of the fact that the Marxist state had failed to achieve its goal of human equality.
4. James Alfred Martin, *The New Dialogue Between Philosophy and Theology* (London: Black, 1966), 27ff. See also Theodosius Dobzhansky, *Mankind Evolving* (New Haven, Conn.: Yale University Press, 1962), 285ff and passim.
5. Isaiah 5:8.
6. Amos 2:6; 6:4–6.
7. Isaiah 1:10ff; 3:15; 59:5–7 and passim.
8. Psalm 24:1. The injunction that flows from this concept is that the land, belonging as it does to God, must never be sold "in perpetuity" (Lev. 25:23). This biblical command was observed in the original policies of the modern Jewish National Fund. Land purchased by the JNF could be used only for socially acceptable purposes. It could not be sold—it could only be leased—and it remained the property of the entire people.
9. According to Brown, Driver, and Briggs, the etymology of the word *yovel* is doubtful. Some scholars connect it with a root meaning "ram," whereas others believe that it had to do with being borne along in procession. In any case, its received meaning is as a title for the fiftieth year. A Yiddish colloquialism for something that occurs rarely is that it happens "once in a *yovel*."
10. Isaiah 56:6f.

11. No human being is excluded from the opportunity to be righteous. The Torah was given in the wilderness so that it might be "free to all who come into the world" (Mechilta Bahodesh V), and Leviticus 18:5 says "which if a person do, he shall live by them." It does not say "priest, Levite, Israelite . . . it says person" (Avodah Zara 3a). Alluding to the fact that even the High Priest is obliged to ask for forgiveness of his sins on the Day of Atonement, Samuel Belkin finds that this act of contrition and confession by the High Priest "demonstrates for all the fundamental concept of Judaism that in the eyes of the law and before God all men are equal . . . to deny that sacredness rests only on one personality [the High Priest] is to affirm the sacredness of every human personality." See Samuel Belkin, *In His Image* (London: Abelard Schuman, 1959), 60ff.

12. Most authorities believe this to be Simon II, who was the High Priest about 200 B.C.E.

13. The Greek name has led some to believe that Antigonos was a convert. However, Greek nomenclature was not uncommon among Jews.

14. Avot I:5.

15. Ibid., v. 6.

16. Ibid., v. 12.

17. Ibid., v. 16.

18. The Torah specified that there must be no discrimination in law. Aliens as well as the native-born are to be equally protected by the legal system (Lev. 24:22; Num. 15:14f). Universal equity is also affirmed. See Joseph Blenkentoff, "The Judge of All the Earth," *Journal of Jewish Studies* XLI, no. 1 (spring 1990).

19. Exodus 23:4f; Proverbs 24:17, 17:5; Proverbs 25:21; quoted in Romans 12:20; and see Midrash Proverbs ad loc. (25:21).

20. Exodus 23:2; Avot II:15.

21. Rashi's comment on Numbers 13:2.

22. Avot II:11.

23. Avot III:10, 14.

24. The word *adam* has the same universal import in Avot IV:1.

25. See note 11 in this chapter.

26. "Rabbi Joshua said to him [to Rabbi Eliezer who held a contrary view] 'there are righteous persons among the nations who will have a share in the world-to-come.'" Tosefta, Sanhedrin

XIII:2, ed. Zuckermandel (Jerusalem: 1928), 434. Also, "There are righteous persons among the pagans (*ov'day kochavim*) who have a share in the world to come."

27. Avot IV:3.

28. See Simon Bernfeld, ed., *The Foundations of Jewish Ethics*, trans. Armin Koller, vol. 1 of *Die Lehren des Judenthums* (New York: Macmillan, 1929), q.v. 161–71.

29. Ibid., 166.

30. In *Proceedings of the 5th International Congress of Free Christianity and Religious Progress* (Berlin, Schoenberg), 131. Cited in Bernfeld, ed., *Foundations of Jewish Ethics*.

31. Seder Eliyahu Rabba, ed. Friedmann, 48. Cited by Arthur Marmorstein, *Studies in Jewish Theology* (London: Oxford University Press, 1950), 128f. Note the implied equality of the sexes despite the gender of the Hebrew pronouns.

Chapter 4

1. Martin Buber, *Israel and the World* (New York: Schocken, 1948), 17. See also p. 57 below.

2. Nicholas was a precursor of Hegel, a man of many parts, who achieved high eminence in the church. His magnificent library of manuscripts and incunabula is reverently maintained in his native village of Kues (Cusa) on the Moselle River.

3. See the tractate Makkot in the Mishna.

4. M. Sanhedrin VII:2; Sanhedrin 52b.

5. Makkot 6b–7a, esp. M. Makkot I:10.

6. Ibid.

7. See David M. Feldman, *Birth Control in Jewish Law* (New York: Hebrew Publishing Company, 1968), 251ff, 297ff.

8. Ibid., 259.

9. *Nefesh* here means person. See Feldman, *Birth Control*, 253. See also Urbach, *The Sages*, 214ff.

10. Feldman, *Birth Control*, 264.

11. Ibid., 112, 144ff.

12. Ibid., 286.

13. In Catholic doctrine, the potential embryo—the conjoined sperm and egg—possesses a soul from the moment of conception. Here we confront a linguistic difficulty. In Hebrew,

one term for "soul" is *n'shama*. Another is *nefesh*, which, though it also means soul, generally means "personhood." In normative Jewish thought, the embryo—indeed, the fetus—is not a *nefesh*. Only after birth, and in some ritual respects not until thirty days after birth, is the newborn viewed as a *nefesh*. But see Urbach, *The Sages*, 220, 234ff, 242.

14. B'reshit Rabbah XLVIII:18 to Genesis 18:9–15 (cf. 17:15–21).
15. Ketubot 16b–17a. See Soncino, p. 92, note 12.
16. Deuteronomy 15:1ff.
17. Deuteronomy 15:9.
18. Shebiith IX:3–4.
19. Fully discussed in Gittin 36a–b.
20. Leviticus 19:36. Note the repetition of the word *tsedek*—meaning here "correct" or "exact": *moznei* (balances) *tsedek, avnay* (weights) *tsedek, eyfa tsedek,* and *hin tsedek. (Eyfa* and *hin* are measures—respectively, dry and liquid.)
21. See Jacob Lauterbach, "Ethics of the Halacha," in his *Rabbinic Essays* (Cincinnati: Hebrew Union College Press, 1951), 259ff.
22. Although it occurs in a different context, the injunction of Jesus to "go the second mile" (Matthew 5:41) invites comparison.
23. Baba Metsia 83a, citing Proverbs 2:20a and 20b. The citation from Proverbs is significant attesting to the fact that by this time (fourth century C.E.) the entire Tanakh was considered Torah.
24. Exodus 22:26f; cf. Deuteronomy 24:10–14. The Hebrew word for "fellow" is *rea,* for which an alternative translation is "neighbor," meaning other human beings—Israelite or non-Israelite (cf. Lev. 19:33f; Num. 9:14).
25. See M. Yoma VIII:6; Yoma 82a. See Belkin, *In His Image*, 97ff.
26. Mark 2:27.
27. Mechilta, Ki Tisa. p. 110, ed. I. H. Weiss (Vienna, 1865). See also Yoma 85b.
28. Sifra. Aḥarey Mot. XIII:14, ed. I. H. Weiss (Vienna, 1863), 106a. Citing Leviticus 18:5.
29. M. Eduyot I:13. See chapter 6, p. 79ff., for a full discussion of the concept of *tikkun olam.*
30. Both these examples of scriptural injunctions that dis-

turbed the rabbinic sages are found in the Torah: the "stubborn and rebellious son" in Deuteronomy 21:18f and the woman suspected of adultery in Numbers 5:12ff. See Tosefta Sanhedrin 11:6, ed. Zuckermandel, 431.

31. The rabbinic solution is found in Sanhedrin 71a. If you interpret it correctly, you nullify it. See my *Unity of the Contraries* (Syracuse, N.Y.: Syracuse University Press, 1984), 6f.

32. Numbers 19:2ff. Numbers Rabbah, Ḥukkat XIX, 5, 8 (Soncino, 755). See also *Pesikta d'Rav Kahana*, Piska 4:1, ed. Bernard Mandelbaum (New York: Jewish Theological Seminary, 1963), 54f.

33. M. Sotah IX:9.

34. Genesis 23.

35. Rashi quoting the *Compendium She'iltot of R. Aḥai Gaon*. Cited in Leo Jung, *Business Ethics in Jewish Law* (New York: Hebrew Publishing Company, 1987), 25.

36. The question of the relationship between buyer and seller is explained in the tractate Baba Metsia 49a–51b. See Jung, p. 22, and compare the spirit of Psalm 15.

37. See Aaron Levine, in Jung, *Business Ethics*, 205ff.

38. Leviticus 19:14. The rabbinic tradition extends the meaning of this verse not only to taking advantage of someone's ignorance, but also tempting to sin. E.g., Pesaḥim 2b. See also Kiddushin 32a; Baba Metsia 5b, 75b, 90b; and Avoda Zara 6a.

39. See Jung, *Business Ethics*, 12ff.

40. Philip Wylie, *Generation of Vipers* (Marietta, Ga.: Larlin Corp., 1978), 142. "It was necessary for them to be honest and decent only with each other. All the rest of mankind was cold turkey, to be preyed upon, cheated, lied to, swindled and knocked on the head, no punishment for gutting a goy." In the 1978 edition, Wylie added the following as a footnote to this passage: "This in its literal sense is an error. I have since read the Talmud [sic!—twenty-three volumes in the Soncino English translation]." Wylie then adds that "psychologically and historically, the assertion holds valid." The entire passage, including the footnote added in later editions, is founded on a falsehood and reeks of anti-Semitism.

41. Isaiah 58:3ff.

42. Levine, in Jung, *Business Ethics*, 5.

43. Rabbinic literature offers more illustrations of this ap-

proach than could be cited, because it is the common format of discussion for the sages. The Aramaic word *p'lugta* and the Hebrew *mahloket*, meaning disagreement or division, could be applied to innumerable passages. Examples of differences leading to resolution are the discussions in Yoma 4b or the Jerusalem Talmud tractate *Peah* I:I–IIIa on defining a minimum measure. Cf. Shabbat 15a, where the dissension between Hillel and Shammai is deemed good and right by reason of their intent (see below).

44. Mishnah Peah I:1. The making of peace between human beings is regarded as an unmeasurable *mitzvah* rewarded in life and in immortality. Citing Psalm 34:15, the Jerusalem Talmud enjoins us to seek peace where we are and to pursue it everywhere else (Y. Peah I:1, 16a).

45. Avot V:17.

46. In his commentary to the Mishnah (ad loc. Avot V:17).

47. See note 52 in this chapter.

48. These terms are used in the Bible in contexts entirely different from the later rabbinical usage: in Amos 9:1 (to divide), in Zech. 4:9 (to carry out), and in Ecclesiastes 8:1, where *pesher* means a solution. See Ira Y. Kasdan for definitions and further reference in *Jewish Action*, spring 1990; "The Torah Way of Justice," in Harav Joseph Soloveitchik, *Reflections of the Rav* (Jerusalem: World Zionist Organization, 1979), and the articles by Menachem Elon in *The Principles of Jewish Law* (Jerusalem: Keter Publishing House, 1975). I am grateful to attorney Gerald S. Clay of Honolulu for having called to my attention this whole area of Halachah and the procedures deriving from the rabbinic discussion in Talmud and the responsa literature (see bibliography following notes section).

49. Sanhedrin 66a. See Menachem Elon, "Compromise," in *Principles of Jewish Law*, 570ff.

50. Deuteronomy 1:17.

51. Yad (Mishneh Torah) Sanhedrin 22:4. Cited also in *Shulchan Aruch,* Hoshen Mishpat, 12.2.

52. Soloveitchik, *Reflections of the Rav*, 53–54.

53. The danger inherent in oaths is expressed in many stories and in several different ethnic mythological sources. A dramatic, tragic example is the story of Jephthah's oath resulting in the death of his daughter (Judges 11:30ff). Cf. the story of Agamemnon and Iphigenia in the parallel Greek myth. See Elmer

Klinger, "Oaths and Vows," in the *Encyclopedia of Religion*, vol. 15 (New York: Macmillan, 1987). See also the article "Vows," *Hastings Encyclopedia of Religion and Ethics*, vol. 12, esp. Morris Joseph, 657ff (New York, 1921).
54. Deuteronomy 16:20; Sanhedrin 32b.
55. Zechariah 8:16. See Elon, *Principles of Jewish Law*, 572.
56. Sanhedrin 6b. Steinsaltz in his "modern commentary" places the word *peshara* in parentheses after the word *bitzua*. See note 48 above, and corresponding text.
57. Soloveitchik, *Reflections of the Rav*, 56.
58. Avot III:15. See beginning of chapter 4, note 1.
59. Buber, *Israel and the World*, 17. Leviticus Rabba X:1. Also Pesikta d'Rav Kahana, Piska 19:3 (Mandelbaum, 304). (Levine, in Jung's *Business Ethics*, quotes Dr. Joseph Wohlgemuth as having defined this "unity" as *"liebevolle Gerechtigkeit*: love-filled justice.")
60. Jung, *Business Ethics*, 24. The dual meaning of the word *tsedek* is made plain in Leviticus 19:15, where it connotes both righteousness and impartiality. See Jung, *Business Ethics*, 9f.
61. Exodus 34:6f.
62. See *Siddur: The Traditional Prayer Book*, ed. David de Sola Pool (New York: Behrman House, 1960), 237, 238.

Chapter 5

1. Grandson or great-grandson of Hillel the Elder. Head of the Academy. See chapter 4, p. 44.
2. Kiddushin 40b. "Rabbi Tarfon and the Elders were once reclining in the upper story of Nitza's house in Lydda [see Soncino translation, Sanhedrin, p. 502, note 3] when this question was raised before them: Is study greater, or practice? Rabbi Tarfon said, practice is greater. Rabbi Akiba said, study for it leads to practice. Then they all answered and said, Great is Torah when it leads to action." Note how the consensus resolves the conflict with a "both-and." The problem phrased in Christian thought as "faith versus works" becomes "study versus deeds" in rabbinic discussion.
3. *The Sh'ma Yisrael* ("Hear, O Israel"), Deuteronomy 6:4–9.

The pious Jew recites the Sh'ma three times daily, as well as at high moments of religious observance and as a death-bed confession.

4. M. Berachot II:2.
5. *Duties of the Heart: Hovot Ha-l'vavot.* IV, 2–3.
6. For the problem of the authorship of the Epistle of James, see Bo Reike, Introduction to Anchor Bible Edition (New York: Doubleday, 1964).
7. Lauterbach, "Ethics of the Halacha," 259ff.
8. See my *Social Relevance of the Eighth-Century Prophets,* 12. Also Sheldon Blank, *Jeremiah* (H.U.C. Press, 1961), esp. 50ff. On the death of Isaiah, see Urbach, *The Sages,* 559.
9. *Mitzvot Aniyim* in the *Yad Hazakah* (*Mishneh Torah*), Treatise II, Chap. VIII, par. 11, trans. Israel Klein (New Haven, Conn.: Yale University Press, 1979), 83.
10. Leviticus 19:9f; cf. Deuteronomy 24:19–22.
11. See below, p. 67.
12. A delightfully playful sidelight on *shik'cha* is afforded by some verse written by Helen Lukas Engle, the sister of Claude G. Montefiore. See Montefiore and Loewe, *Rabbinic Anthology,* 192. This is what Ms. Engle wrote (*The Jewish Year,* 2d ed. [London: Rutledge, 1926], 166):

> Blessed art Thou, O Lord, whose gracious will enables me thy bidding to fulfill even through some oversight.

The command in the Torah (Deuteronomy 24:19–20) is clear:

"If when you are harvesting your field you forget [*shachakta*] a sheaf . . . you shall not go back to take it. It is to be left for the stranger [alien], the orphan and the widow . . ." The sages make the same point that Ms. Engle expressed in light verse. The Tosefta puts it in the form of a story about a *Hasid* who forgot a sheaf and rejoicing in his having forgotten, instructs his son to bring a bullock for a burnt offering and a bullock for a whole offering and when his son asks why this celebration, the *Hasid* replies: "All the commandments in the Torah were given us by God to be observed knowingly, but this one we can observe only unknowingly. If we seek to keep it deliberately, it cannot be kept. It is ordained only for forgetfulness." Tos. Peah III:8, ed. Zuckermandel, p. 22.

13. Compare contemporary practice in restaurant and hotel buffet tables, where the same rule usually applies.

14. See W. Gunther Plaut, *The Torah: A Modern Commentary* (New York: Union of American Hebrew Congregations, 1981), 1443.

15. The Gleaning Network of Central Point, Oregon, collects one million pounds of unharvested fruits and vegetables each year for distribution to the poor (*New York Times,* 22 September 1990).

16. M. Shekalim V:6.

17. Baba Bathra 9b. See Proverbs 21:14. The question of almsgiving and the injunctions to *ts'daka* ("righteousness" or "charity") is given full attention in Baba Bathra 8a–10a.

18. Ronald Green, *Religion and Moral Reason,* 173. For an excellent survey on aid to the poor in Jewish practice, see pp. 169–74 of this presentation.

19. M. Peah I:2.

20. See Ketubot 67b–68a, where these concepts are illustrated in several anecdotes—some of which are humorous or "tongue-in-cheek," such as the story of a poor man who applied to Raba for help. "What do you usually eat?" Rabba asked him. "Fat chicken and old wine," the man replied. Whereupon Raba said, "Don't you consider this a burden on the community?" The man replied, "I don't eat what is theirs. I eat what the All-Merciful provides for me." And he quoted Psalm 145:15, "Thou givest them their food in due season," meaning that the Holy One provides food for every individual according to his habits and his needs. At that moment, Raba's sister, who had not seen Raba for thirteen years, came and brought him a fat chicken and old wine. "See?" said the mendicant, "that's just what I said!" Then Raba said, "I apologize to you. Come and eat!" The arrogance of Jewish mendicants, immortalized in Israel Zangwill's *King of Shnorrers,* stems from their conviction that they are giving those to whom they apply, the opportunity to do a *mitzvah.*

This same page of the Talmud contains the story that a formerly wealthy man who had come down in the world came to Hillel for assistance. Because the man had been accustomed to riding on a horse with a servant running before him, Hillel hired a horse and a servant for him. When he was unable to find a

servant, Hillel himself ran before him for three miles! See Cronbach, "Philanthropy in Rabbinic Literature," in *Religion in Its Social Setting* (Cincinnati: Hebrew Union College Press, 1933), 106f. Dr. Cronbach's essay is both detailed and definitive, recording what the rabbinic sources say about aid to the poor.
21. E.g., *Sh'mot Rabba* XXXI:4. Cf. Baba Bathra 9b: "He who gives a small coin to a poor man obtains six blessings [Isaiah 58:8–9] but he who addresses to him comforting words obtains eleven blessings [Isaiah 58:10–12]."
22. *Mishneh Torah, Mat'not Aniyim*, Book VII, Treatise II, esp. VII: 2, 3, 7, 10. Cf. note 3 in chap. 1.
23. See note 20 above.
24. *Mishneh Torah*, IX:3.
25. *Mishneh Torah*, X:7ff.
26. Baba Metzia IIIa. According to Raba, "Oppression and robbery are identical." Scripture divides them, he says, in order to teach us that withholding the wages of a hired laborer transgresses *two* negative commands of the Torah.
27. The biblical attitude toward slaves is centered in the repeated injunction to "remember that you were slaves in Egypt." See above, p. 29f. Cf. Leviticus 25:43, 46, 53; Deuteronomy 23:15, 16. (In this instance the reference is to any slave, Hebrew or alien.) See Jeremiah 34:15ff. In the rabbinic literature, the legal ramifications of the subject are complex and frequently disturbing to modern sensibilities when taken out of their context. They are contained in discussions that are hermeneutical in character and most often moot (see *Encyclopedia Judaica*, "Slavery," vol. 14, 1655ff). But the tendency to regard the slave with the respect due all human beings breaks through the legalisms— e.g., Rabbi Joshua ben Levi advises that if one has a nubile daughter, he should free his slave that he may marry her (Pesaḥim 113a). Our earlier reference to the slave who was half-free and given full freedom so as to be able to marry (see M. Gittin IV:5) reflects the same humane view.

The Hebrew slave is to be on a par with his master in food and drink (Kiddushin 15a); injury to a slave, alien as well as Hebrew, results in liberation (Kiddushin 24a–25a). But the spirit of the tradition and the normative view is expressed by Maimonides in the summary with which he concludes his discussion of the subject (*Mishneh Torah*, Book XII, Treatise V; *Avadim* IX:8. trans. Isaac Klein, *The Book of Acquisitions* [New Haven, Conn.: Yale University Press, 1951], 281):

> It is permitted to work a heathen slave with rigor. Though such is the rule, it is the quality of piety and the way of wisdom that a man be merciful and pursue justice and not make his yoke heavy upon the slave or distress him, but give him to eat and to drink of all foods and drinks. The Sages of old were wont to let the slave partake of every dish that they themselves ate of and to give the meal of the cattle and of the slaves precedence over their own . . . Thus the master should not disgrace them by hand or by word; scriptural law has delivered them only unto slavery and not unto disgrace. Nor should he heap upon the slave oral abuse and anger but should rather speak to him softly and listen to his claims.
>
> So it is explained in the good paths of Job . . . : "If I did despise the cause of my manservant or of my maidservant, when they contended with me . . . Did not He that made me in the womb make him?" (Job 31:13, 15)

28. Genesis 1:28. See the Midrash Rabbah to Ecclesiastes 7:13, which expands the biblical idea: "When God created the first human beings, He led them around the Garden of Eden and said, 'Look at My works! See how beautiful they are . . . I created them all for your care. See to it that you do not spoil or destroy My world . . .'"

29. M. Baba Bathra II:8,9.

30. Deuteronomy 23:12ff.

31. Sifre 203 to Deuteronomy 20:19, ed. Louis Finkelstein (New York: Jewish Theological Seminary, 1969), 237.

32. Norman Lamm, "Ecology in Jewish Law and Theology," in *Faith and Doubt* (New York: K'tav, 1970), 162–85.

33. *Essen täg*—"eating days"—is a Yiddish expression denoting the custom by which the householders in Jewish communities undertook to provide dinner, each of them signing up for one day each week, for a *yeshiva bochur*, a Talmud student away from home.

34. See Israel Goldstein's record of the Jewish Court of Ar-

bitration in New York City and the revival of *p'shara* as a viable alternative to litigation in the civil courts. (See chapter 4, note 43.)

35. See Roland Gittlesohn, "Social Action and Civil Rights," in *Retrospect and Prospect*, ed. Bertram Korn (New York: CCAR, 1965).
36. See chapter 3, note 30.
37. Gittelsohn, "Social Action and Civil Rights," 86ff.

Chapter 6

1. See chapter 2, p. 28.
2. Isaiah 4:11.
3. Deuteronomy 7:6–8; Mechilta. Ba-ḥodesh V, line 63ff, ed. Jacob Lauterbach (Philadelphia: Jewish Publication Society, 1933), 234. See also L. Ginsburg, *Legends of the Jews*, vol. VI (Philadelphia: Jewish Publication Society, 1968), 30 n. 181.
4. Ketubot 112a. See Urbach, *The Sages*, 532 (bottom), and Rashi ad loc. The Sadducees were also Jews and, for the most part, were recognized as such. In Talmudic usage, the designation *Sadducee* is frequently a substitution for *Min* (heretic) or Jewish-Christian. See Exodus 24:7. See also Shabbat 88a.
5. Sanhedrin 105a.
6. Biblical scholarship ascribes the servant verses to different hands, but together they convey the *received* image of the servant with its powerful influence on Jewish thought (Isaiah 42:1ff; 58:5ff; 53:1ff).
7. *The Complete Diaries*, 5 vols., ed. Raphael Patai (New York: Herzl Press, Yoseloff, 1960). See vol. II, 581. Quoted in Alex Bern, *Theodore Herzl: A Biography* (Philadelphia: Jewish Publication Society, 1940), 243. An abridgment of the Herzl Diaries in English is also available (New York: Grosset and Dunlap, 1962).
8. See chapter 1, p. 14f.
9. See chapter 4, p. 53.
10. S. D Goitein, "Human Rights in Jewish Thought and Life in the Middle Ages," in *Essays on Human Rights*, ed. David Sidorsky (Philadelphia: Jewish Publication Society, 1979).
11. Ibid., 258f. This description of persistent Jewish faithfulness in alien environments is confirmed by no less an authority than the church father (fourth and fifth centuries) Augustine,

who wrote, "It is in truth a surprising fact that the Jewish people never gave up its laws, either under the rule of pagan kings or under the dominion of Christians. In this respect, it is different from other tribes and nations; no emperor or king who found them in his land was able to prevent the Jews from being differentiated, by their observance of their Law, from the rest of the family of nations." From his *Contra Faustum* (ed. Migne, PL XLII, p. 261). Cited by Urbach, *The Sages*, p. 465 of the Hebrew, p. 524 of the English.

    12. See J. H. Hertz, *Authorized Daily Prayerbook* (New York: 1959), 211ff. Also *Gates of Understanding*, vol. II, ed. Lawrence A. Hoffman (New York: Central Conference of American Rabbis, 1959), 44f. The twelfth-century Holy Day Prayerbook called the *Maḥzor Vitry* contains the complete Hebrew prayer in its present form as found in traditional prayerbooks. A. Z. Idlesohn, *Jewish Liturgy* (New York: Schocken, 1952), 316.

    13. Idlesohn, *Jewish Liturgy*, 316.

    14. Ecclesiastes 1:15; 7:13; 12:9.

    15. B'rachot 48b (Soncino, 292).

    16. See Eugene Lipman, "*Mip'nay Tikkun Ha-Olam* in the Talmud," in *The Life of the Covenant*, ed. Joseph A. Edelheit (Chicago: Spertus College Press, 1986). David Daube (in *Essays on Human Rights*, 243) cites the phrase as the underlying authority for helping slaves to escape. The Bible ordains that an escaped slave may not be returned to his former owner but must be given refuge (Deut. 23:16f). Gittin 38a rules that an escaped slave is declared free. See "Slavery" in the *Encyclopedia Judaica*, vol. XIV, p. 1665f. Also see chapter 5, note 26.

    17. See chapter 4, note 18.

    18. See Lipman, *Mip'nay Tikkun Ha-Olam*, 104ff.

    19. Ibid., 107f.

    20. Herbert Chanan Brichto, "The Hebrew Bible on Human Rights," in *Essays on Human Rights*, ed. David Sidorsky (Philadelphia: Jewish Publication Society, 1979).

    21. See Joan G. Roland, *Jews in British India* (Brandeis University Press/University Press of New England, 1989), 76f.

    22. Song of Songs I:5. The King James translation "I am black *but* I am beautiful" is not warranted by the Hebrew text. Marvin Pope has an extended comment on this in his note ad loc. *The Song of Songs*, Anchor Bible edition (New York: Doubleday, 1977).

23. See Seth Cagan and Philip Dray, *We Are Not Afraid* (New York: Macmillan, 1988). Also my "Mississippi Memoir," in *Manna* (Reform Synagogues of Great Britain Quarterly, London), summer 1988.

24. Goitein, "Human Rights in Jewish Thought and Life," 263.

25. See Kevin Phillips, *The Politics of Rich and Poor* (New York: Random House, 1990). Phillips maintains that in the 1980s, the rich were favored by government policy and hence got richer, while the real incomes of the lower middle class and blue-collar workers declined. Without factoring in the effect of inflation, which dramatically reduced the value of the dollar, the hourly wage of production workers rose from $6,370 in 1968 to $11,735 in 1988 while the total compensation of corporate chief executives, which averaged $157,000 in 1968, reached an average figure of $773,000 in 1988.

26. Deuteronomy 15:11.

27. Numbers 27.

28. Exodus 38:11ff. See Mark Zborowski and Elizabeth Herzog, *Life Is with People* (New York: Schocken, 1962), 131–32.

29. Brichto, "Hebrew Bible on Human Rights," 277f.

30. Goitein, "Human Rights in Jewish Thought and Life," 255.

31. Avot I:12.

32. See Judah Goldin, *The Fathers According to Rabbi Nathan* (New Haven: Yale University Press, 1955), 67.

33. This underlies the seeming oxymoron that ocurs in the English translation when David asks Uriah the Hittite (2 Samuel 11:7) concerning the *sh'lom ha-milḥama*—which means "How is the battle going?"—not "What is the peace of the war?"

34. See Dorff, 8ff.

35. See above, p. 85.

36. Gittin 59b. See Cronbach, "War and Peace in Jewish Tradition," *Yearbook of the Central Conference of American Rabbis*, vol. XLVI (New York: Central Conference of American Rabbis, 1989). See also Yebamot 109a (bottom), 109b.

37. Deuteronomy 20:8.

38. M. Sotah VIII:5. According to some commentators, he is afraid of committing *additional* transgressions.

39. M. Shabbat VI:4.

40. For a helpful survey of peace encomia in Jewish liturgy and literature, see Aryeh Lova Eliav, *New Heart, New Spirit* (Philadelphia: Jewish Publication Society, 1988), esp. 165–71.

41. Ernst Bloch, *Man on His Own* (New York: Herder and Herder, 1970). Especially Cox, 7ff, and Moltmann, 19ff, on "The Principle of Hope."

42. Isaiah 43:19.

43. Psalm 126.

44. Translated by Maurice Samuel, in *A Golden Treasury of Jewish Literature,* ed. Leo Schwarz (New York: Holt Rinehart, 1937), 624.

Epilogue

1. See above, p. 87.

2. There is a remarkable series of negative statements on the generation of the Messiah in Sanhedrin 97a, 98a, 98b. The generation will have "the face of a dog," impudence will increase, there will be an abundance of informers . . . and so on.

3. Avot d'Rabbi Natan 33b–34a. Cited by Urbach, *The Sages,* 667. (Hebrew ed., 600). Cf. Habakkuk II:3.

4. "Bit by bit"—*Kiuema, Kiuema.* Y. Berachot I:2c Cited by Urbach, *The Sages,* 678 (Hebrew ed., 60a).

5. Sanhedrin 98a.

6. Sanhedrin 97b.

7. *Siddur,* ed. J. H. Hertz (New York: Bloch, 1960), 10a.

Bibliography

Values: Problems of Definition

Dewey, John. "Field of Value." In *Value: A Cooperative Inquiry*, edited by Ray Lepley. New York: Columbia University Press, 1949.

Garnett, A. Campbell. "Critique of John Dewey's 'Field of Value.'" In *Value: A Cooperative Inquiry*, edited by Ray Lepley. New York: Columbia University Press, 1949.

Green, Ronald M. *Religion and Moral Reason*. New York: Oxford University Press, 1988.

Hare, R. M. *The Language of Morals*. London: Oxford University Press, 1961.

Hartmann, Robert. "The Science of Values." In *New Knowledge in Human Values*, edited by Abraham H. Maslow. New York: Harper, 1959.

Lelyveld, Arthur J. "Transient Isms and Abiding Values." In *Tradition and Contemporary Experience*, edited by Alfred Jospe. New York: Schocken Books, 1970.

———. "A Distinctive Value Stance." *Journal of Reform Judaism*, fall 1978.

Lepley, Ray, ed. *Value: A Cooperative Inquiry*. New York: Columbia University Press, 1949.

Margenau, Henry. "The Scientific Role of Value Theory." In *New Knowledge in Human Values*, edited by Abraham H. Maslow. New York: Harper, 1959.

Maslow, Abraham H., ed. *New Knowledge in Human Values*. New York: Harper, 1959.

Perry, Ralph Barton. *Realms of Value*. Cambridge, Mass.: Harvard University Press. 1954.

Tillich, Paul. "Is a Science of Human Values Possible?" In *New Knowledge in Human Values*, edited by Abraham H. Maslow. New York: Harper, 1959.

Traditional Jewish Sources: Bible and Rabbinics

(Biblical and rabbinic references are found in the notes. See also Note on Classical Sources at the end of this bibliography.)

Belkin, Samuel. *In His Image*. London: Abelard Schuman, 1959.
Bernfeld, Simon, ed. *The Foundation of Jewish Ethics*, translated by Armin Koller. Vol. 1 of *Die Lehren des Judenthums*. New York: Macmillan, 1929.
Bernfeld, Simon. *Die Sittlichen Pflichten der Gemeinschaft* ("Moral Communal Duties," untranslated). Berlin, 1923.
Borowitz, Eugene. "Ḥillul Hashem: A Universal Rubric in Halachic Ethics." In *The Life of the Covenant*, edited by Joseph A. Edelheit. Chicago: Spertus College Press, 1988.
Carmody, Denise, and John Carmody. *Ways to the Center*. Belmont, Calif.: Wadsworth Publishing Co., 1989. Pages 260 to 301 offer a competent and fair description of Judaism's beliefs and practices.
Cronbach, Abraham. *The Bible and Our Social Outlook*. New York: Union of American Hebrew Congregations, 1941. Topically dated but contains significant insights.
———. "Philanthropy in Rabbinic Literature." In *Religion in Its Social Setting*. Cincinnati: Hebrew Union College Press, 1933. A definitive survey.
———. "War and Peace in Jewish Tradition." In *Yearbook of the Central Conference of American Rabbis*, vol. XLVI. New York: Central Conference of American Rabbis, 1989.
Edelheit, Joseph A., ed. *The Life of the Covenant* (essays in honor of Rabbi Hermann Schaalmann). Chicago: Spertus College Press, 1988.
Elon, Menachem, ed. *The Principles of Jewish Law*. Jerusalem: Keter Publishing House, 1975.
Feldman, David M. *Birth Control in Jewish Law*. New York: Hebrew Publishing Company, 1968.
Israel, Richard. "Jewish Tradition and Political Action." In *The Jewish Heritage Reader*. New York: Taplinger Publishing Company, 1965.
Jacobs, Louis. *Jewish Values*. London: Vallentine, Mitchell, 1960.
Jung, Leo. *Business Ethics in Jewish Law*. With an extended addendum on contemporary relevance by Aaron Levine. New York: Hebrew Publishing Company, 1987.

Kadushin, Max. *The Rabbinic Mind*. New York: Jewish Theological Seminary, 1952.
Konvitz, Milton R., ed. *Judaism and Human Rights*. New York: W. W. Norton, 1972.
Lauterbach, Jacob. "Ethics of the Halacha." In *Rabbinic Essays*. Cincinnati: Hebrew Union College Press, 1951.
Lazaron, Moris S. "A Non-Pacifist Point of View." In *Yearbook of the Central Conference of American Rabbis*, vol. XLVI. New York: Central Conference of American Rabbis, 1989.
Lelyveld, Arthur. *The Social Relevance of the Eighth Century Prophets*. Cincinnati: Hebrew Union College Press, 1973.
———. *Spokesmen of God*. In *The Jewish Heritage Reader*. New York: Taplinger Publishing Company, 1965.
———. *The Unity of the Contraries*. Syracuse, N.Y.: Syracuse University Press, 1984.
Lipman, Eugene. "*Mipne Tikkun Ha-Olam* in the Talmud." In *The Life of the Covenant*, edited by Joseph A. Edelheit. Chicago: Spertus College Press, 1988. Explores a talmudic usage that differs from the contemporary normative interpretation.
Maimonides (Rabbi Moshe ben Maimon). *Mishneh Torah* (or *Yad Ḥazakah*) Code of Jewish Law. Section on hiring and gifts to the poor *(Mat'not Aniyim)*. Edited by Philip Birnbaum. New York: Hebrew Publishing Company. Also Yale University Press edition (1949), Bk. VII, 45ff.
Meyerowitz, Arthur. *Social Ethics of the Jews*. New York: Bloch, 1935.
Montefiore, C. G., and H. Loewe, eds. *A Rabbinic Anthology*. London: Macmillan, 1938.
Neusner, Jacob. *Formative Judaism*. Brown University Judaic Studies no. 37. Chico, Calif.: Scholars Press, 1982. See esp. p. 45ff, "The Quest for the Historical Hillel."
———. *First-Century Judaism in Crisis*. New York: K'tav, 1982.
———. *The Social Study of Judaism*. Brown Judaic Studies no. 160. Atlanta: Scholars Press, 1982.
Sicker, Martin. *The Judaic State: A Study in Rabbinic Political Theory*. New York: Praeger, 1988.
Silberman, Lou. "Ethos and Ethics in Rabbinic Judaism." In *The Life of the Covenant*, edited by Joseph A. Edelheit. Chicago: Spertus College Press, 1988.
Soloveitchik, Joseph. *Reflections of the Rav*. Jerusalem: World Zionist Organization, 1979.

Urbach, Ephraim. *The Sages: Their Concepts and Beliefs.* Jerusalem: Magnes Press, 1975. See the Hebrew original for footnotes. Jerusalem 1969.

Wigoder, Geoffrey, ed. *Jewish Values.* Jerusalem: Keter Publishing, 1974. A collection of relevant articles from the *Encyclopedia Judaica.*

Social Values in Contemporary Jewish Thought

Borowitz, Eugene. *Choices in Modern Jewish Thought.* New York: Behrman, 1983.

Brichto, Herbert Chanan. "The Hebrew Bible on Human Rights." In *Essays on Human Rights,* edited by David Sidorsky. Philadelphia: Jewish Publication Society, 1979.

Buber, Martin. *Israel and the World.* New York: Schocken, 1948.

Dorff, Elliot. *A Time for War and a Time for Peace.* A Jewish Perspective on the Ethics of International Intervention. Los Angeles: University of Judaism, 1987.

Eliav, Arie Lova. *New Heart, New Spirit.* Biblical Humanism for Modern Israel. Philadelphia: Jewish Publication Society, 1988.

Fishman, Sylvia Barack. *A Breath of Life: Feminism in the American Jewish Community.* New York: The Free Press, 1993.

Gittelsohn, Roland. "Social Action and Civil Rights." In *Retrospect and Prospect,* edited by Bertram Korn. New York: Central Conference of American Rabbis, 1965.

Goitein, S. D. "Human Rights in Jewish Thought and Life in the Middle Ages." In *Esays on Human Rights,* edited by David Sidorsky. Philadelphia: Jewish Publication Society, 1979.

Gordis, Robert. *Judaic Ethics for a Lawless World.* New York: Jewish Theological Seminary, 1986.

Greenberg, Elie. *On Women and Judaism: A View from Tradition.* Philadelphia: Jewish Publication Society, 1981.

Heschel, Susannah, ed. *On Being a Jewish Feminist.* New York: Schocken Books, 1983.

Kuzik, Alfred J. *Social Work and Jewish Values.* Washington, D.C.: Public Affairs Press, 1959.

Lamm, Norman. *The Good Society.* New York: Viking Press, 1974.

———. "Ecology in Jewish Law and Theology." In *Faith and Doubt.* New York: K'tav, 1970.

Lelyveld, Arthur. *Atheism Is Dead.* Cleveland: World Publishing, 1968.

———. "Mississippi Memoir." *Manna* (Reform Synagogues of Great Britain Quarterly, London), summer 1988.

Meiselman, Moshe. *Jewish Woman in Jewish Law.* New York: K'tav, 1978.

Pogrebin, Letty Cottin. *Deborah, Golda, and Me: Being Female and Jewish in America.* New York: Crown Publishers, 1991.

Priesand, Sally. *Judaism and the New Woman.* New York: Behrman House, 1975.

Schulweiss, Harold M. "The Single Mirror of Jewish Images—The Pluralistic Character of Jewish Ethics." Los Angeles: University of Judaism, 1982.

Sidorsky, David, ed. *Essays on Human Rights.* Philadelphia: Jewish Publication Society, 1979.

St. John, Robert. *Jews, Justice, and Judaism.* New York: Doubleday, 1969. See chapters 19 and 24.

Miscellaneous References

Bloch, Ernst, ed. *Man on His Own.* New York: Herder and Herder, 1970.

Cohen, Steven. *The Dimensions of Jewish Liberalism.* New York: American Jewish Committee, 1989.

Dobzhansky, Theodosius. *Mankind Evolving.* New Haven: Yale University Press, 1963.

Klausner, Samuel. "Jewry's Survival in a Time of Depopulation." In *Yearbook of the Central Conference of American Rabbis,* vol. XCIX. New York: Central Conference of American Rabbis, 1989.

Langer, Suzanne. *Philosophy in a New Key.* Cambridge, Mass.: Harvard University Press, 1942.

Martin, James Alfred. *The New Dialogue Between Philosophy and Theology.* London: Black, 1966.

Wheelwright, Philip. *The Burning Fountain.* Bloomington: Indiana University Press, 1959.

Zborowski, Mark, and Elizabeth Herzog. *Life Is with People.* New York: Schocken, 1962.

Note on Classical Sources

Rabbinic literature cited in the text falls for the most part into three different categories: Mishnah, Gemara, and Midrash. Mishnah, meaning "study," is written in classical Hebrew and came into its final form about

200 C.E. (Common Era; equivalent to A.D.). Its editing is attributed to Rabbi Yehudah ha-Nasi (Judah the Presiding Officer) and it is largely the product of the academy at Yavneh (70 C.E. to 200 C.E.). The Mishnah is divided into six topical "orders," and those orders are in turn divided into sixty-three "tractates."

The references to the Mishnah usually cite tractate, chapter and verse. Gemara (completion) is the recorded discussions (mostly in Aramaic) of the Mishnah. Mishnah and Gemara together make up "Talmud" ("learning").

There are two Talmuds, one completed in the land of Israel and called "Yerushalmi," usually distinguished by the letter Y; the other, larger and more authoritative, completed in Babylon and called "Babli." References to the Gemara of the Babli are to the two-sided page, obverse marked "a" and reverse marked "b." The standard English translation of the Talmud is the one published by the Soncino Press. There is also a very good English translation of Mishnah by Canon Herbert Danby.

Midrash (homiletical exposition) is the term for an extensive literature of interpretation and exposition. Chief within it is the Midrash Rabba, or "Great Midrash," to the five books of the Pentateuch and the five scrolls associated with the festive and "commemorative" holy days. References to them are distinguished by the abbreviation *R*, for Rabba. These also appear in English translations by the Soncino Press. Other Midrashim in the text are Mechilta, Sifra, Sifre, and Seder Eliyahu Rabba. *Specific references to all of these appear in the notes and in the bibliography.* Associated with Mishnah is the Tosefta ("Addendum"). See for example p. 104 top. Other works referred to are the Pesikta d'Rav Kahana, Bachya's Hovot Ha-L'vavot, Maimonides' Yad or Mishneh Torah, and the Shulḥan Aruch (see Index).

Index

abortion, 45–46
Abraham, 51; and Sara, 46, 58
Akiba, 26, 40, 44, 57, 64, 89, 106
Amos, 80–81, 89–90
Avot, 38–40, 93

Bachya ibn Pakuda, 64
Baeck, Leo, 2–3, 33
Bar Kochba, 80, 89–90
Belkin, Samuel, 101
Bellow, Saul, 31
Ben Azzai, 25
bitsuah, 56
bitter water (*sotah*), 51
Blenkentoff, Joseph, 101
Bloch, Ernst, 87
Brichto, Herbert, 84, 112
Buber, Martin, 5, 43, 56, 57
Bull, Nina, 16

capital punishment, 43–45
casuistry, 53–54, 59
caveat emptor, 51–52
Chavez, Cesar, 73
civil rights, 73
concern for others, 8

conflict resolution, 54–55
conscientious objection, 85
contraception, 45; sin of Onan, 45
converts, 2, 37
Cronbach, Abraham, 35, 109, 113
Cusanus, Nicholas, 43

Daube, David, 112
David, 86
Dewey, John: empirical-naturalistic foundation for values, 10; values as "behavioral," 10, 15

ecological concerns, 69–70; *bal tashhit*—"you shall not destroy," 70
Einhorn, David, 72
Eleazar ben Azariah, 44
Eleazar ben Zadok, 44
Eliav, Aryeh Lova, 114
Eliezer ben Yose, 55
Elijah, 91
Elon, Menahem, 105
emunah, 89
Engle, Helen Lukas, 107

121

ensoulment, 102–3
equality, 33, 34–35; Kantian view, 34; of opportunity, 34, 40
equity (*tsedek*), 52, 59
eschatology, this-worldly, 79

Fein, Leonard, 73
Felsenthal, Bernard, 72

Garnett, A. Campbell: critique of Dewey, 11; nature of good, 11
Geiger, Abraham, 41
Gershom of Mayence, 78
Ginsburg, Louis, 111
Gittlesohn, Roland, 111
g'nevat da-at, 52
God: image of, 69; "prays," 60
Goitein, S. D., 78, 82, 84
Green, Ronald, 66, 99, 108
Greenberg, Hayyim, 2

Hanina ben Dosa, 39
Hartman, Robert, 13
Herzl, Theodore, 77
Hillel, 27, 38, 39, 47, 85, 106, 108–9; Bet Hillel (school of), 49–50
Hirsch, Emil G., 41, 72
Hitler, Adolf, 32
Hiyya the Great, 90
Hoffman, Lawrence, 112
hope, 87

Idlesohn, A. Z., 112
Isaiah of Jerusalem, 24, 28, 35, 36, 89; Second Isaiah, 76, 87

Jephthah's daughter, 105
Jesus: ethic of, 8, 49; the great commandment, 29; and the Pharisees, 8
Jewish National Fund, 100
Joseph, Morris, 106
Joshua ben Korha, 55
Joshua ben Levi, 109
Jubilee, 36–37
Judah and Tamar, 83
Judaism: response to whole of life (*kiddush ha-ḥayyim*), 3, 75; sanctifying the everyday, 4, 27–28, 60
Jung, Leo, 53, 59, 60

kadosh, 22–24
kiddush, 29
kiddush ha-shem, 27–28
Klinger, Elmer, 105–6

Lamm, Norman, 110
Langer, Suzanne, 18
Lauterbach, Jacob, 64, 103
Levi ben Yosef, 25, 40
Lipmann, Eugene, 80

Mahpela, cave of, 51
Maimonides, 55, 65, 67–68, 110
Margenau, Henry: antecedent command, 14–15; on religion as outmoded source of values, 15; validation in the group, 15, 77
Martin, James, 34
martyrdom, 99
matan b'seter (one who gives secretly), 66

Mentschlichkeit, 39
Micah, 85, 89
minority opinions, 2, 37
Mishnat Ḥasidim, 48
mitzvah, 5, 14, 21–22, 63, 64
Moltmann, Jürgen, 87
monogamy, 78
Murray, Gilbert, 23, 97
Murray, Robert, 97

Nagel, Ernest, 32
Nahman ben Isaac, 26, 76
Nahum Ish Gam Zu, 7–8
Neusner, Jacob, 98
Nietzsche, Friedrich, 12; cf. Nazi ideology, 17, 32

oaths, vows, 56, 105
Obadiah of Bertinoro, 54
oshek (oppression), 69, 73
Otto, Rudolf, 22

peace (*shalom*), 84–85, 86
peah, leket, shik'cha, 65–66, 67
Perry, Ralph Barton, 13; and Quakers, 13
pesharah, 55
pikuaḥ nefesh (saving life), 49
Plaut, W. Gunther, 108
prophets, 17, 28, 35–36, 64
prosbul, 47
Proverbs, 83

rabbis: heirs of the prophets, 37, 64; oral tradition, 37; skepticism re Messiah, 91
Rachmanim b'ne rachmanim, 50
racism, 87
red heifer, 50–51

religious responses: theodical calculus, escape, pragmatic, 4
ritual, as reminder and transmitter, 30

Samaritan, 8
sanctity of life, 8, 49, 85
Seder, Passover festive meal, 29
servant (in Second Isaiah), 76
shalom (as total well-being), 54, 85
Shammai, 27, 38, 39; Bet Shammai (school of), 49–50
Shim'on ben Gamaliel, 44, 63
Shim'on ben Shetah, 28
Sh'ma (Deuteronomy 6:2 and following), 3, 64, 106–7
Sh'mita, 47
Simon the Just (Shim'on Ha-Tsaddik), 38
slavery, the injunction to remember, 29–30, 109–10, 112
social betterment, 1, 5–6
social services, institutions, 70–71
Solomon ben Judah, 82
Soloveitchik, Joseph, 55–56
stubborn and rebellious son, 50

Tarfon, 44, 64, 106
Tchernichovski, Saul, 88
tikkun olam, 30, 50, 73, 75, 79–80, 82

Tillich, Paul, 13–14, 31
ts'daka (almsgiving), 66–67

values: absolutes, 12, 13; adaptation and efficiency, 12, 13; axiology, 12–13; definition, 9–10, 15, 19; normative, 1–2, 3, 5; posture, 16; stance, 2, 15–16, 17; untranslatables, 18

Wise, Stephen S., 72
women's rights, 82–83
Wylie, Philip, 53

Yehosh'ua, 39
Yiddish, 20
Yoḥanan ben Zakkai, 51
Yose ben Yoḥanan, 38

Zangwill, Israel, 108
Zephaniah, 89